D0921385

THE MYTH OF CERTAINTY

...and other great news

BRIAN PERRY

ISBN: 978-1-54392-402-2 (print)
ISBN: 978-1-54392-403-9 (ebook)

Cover design by Sonia Tetlow
Front cover photo by Mallory Edwards
Back cover photo by Crystal Turnblom
For additional information, please go to yesbrianperry.com

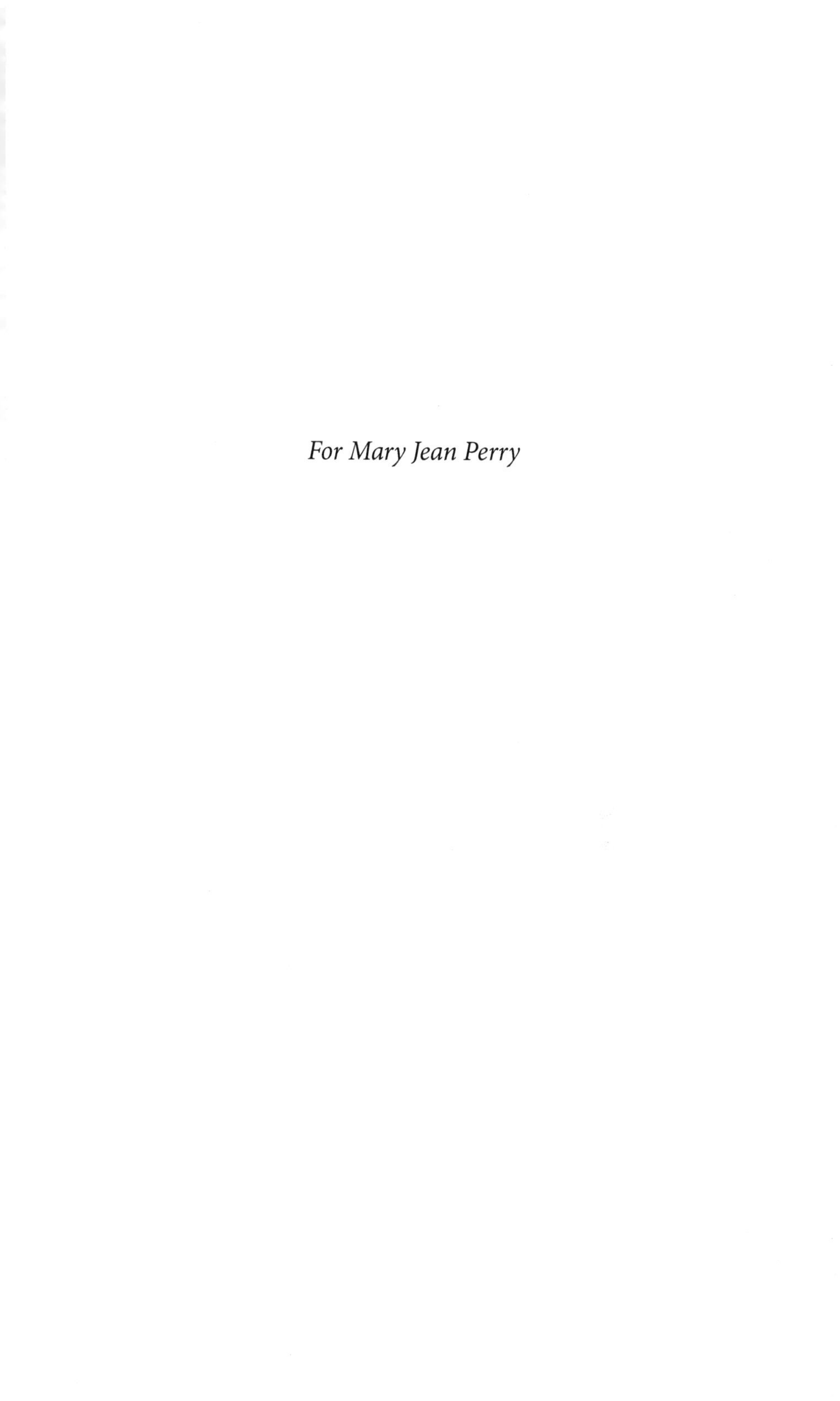

For Mary Jean Perry

Dear Reader,

Thank you, in advance, for opening yourself to the pages ahead. It's been more than a year since I penned the last words of the epilogue, and I keep rewriting this book. I guess that's still on account of how I keep rewriting my life or rather life keeps rewriting me. Do you know the old adage about if you pray for patience prepare to be tested? Yeah, well I decided to write a book about embracing uncertainty. Guess what happened next? Yep. That. Lots of that. And what a gift it has been and continues to be, uncomfortable to be sure but a gift nevertheless.

As I have worked to grow into the thoughts and beliefs I've shared within these pages, my life has given me ample opportunities to put up or shut up. I'm happy to report that I find myself at every turn embracing the richness of the moment more, and more easily and consistently surrendering to both the joy and the pain knowing they will pass. Unavoidably. I am more convinced everyday that this is the way life is and so my task remains unchanged. To stop clinging to the myth of certainty and start embracing the gifts the immovable fact of uncertainty comes bearing.

I was recently reading a book called *The Art of Happiness* by the Dalai Lama and Dr. Howard C. Cutler. Early in its pages, I found a passage relevant in welcoming you to, and setting the stage for, our time together. In the book they are discussing the Western approach to psychology and the unconscious but it feels like a reasonable leap to our topic here as well, that topic being our propensity for constantly betting on the next thing, betting on certainty itself. The Dalai Lama is quoted as saying:

> "It's a bit like you've lost something and you decide that the object is in this room. And once you've decided this, then you've already fixed your parameters; you've precluded the possibility of its being

outside the room or in another room. So you keep on searching and searching, but you are not finding it, yet you continue to assume that it is still hidden in the room!"

That's at the core of what ultimately compelled me to write this handbook. Without yet articulating it as such, I think in the midst of my cycles of suffering and bliss I had the nagging sense the peace and happiness I seek wasn't in the "room" I kept tossing over and over again demanding that it be in. I had the nagging sense I needed to adjust the scope of my search, to look outside of the room. And there, perched like Alice's Cheshire Cat, sat uncertainty smiling gleefully, mischievously asking what took me so long.

And now there's this book, at least that's what I'm calling it as I make final adjustments and prepare to print it and get it into your hands. I have endeavored to stay as true as possible to what I wrote originally, to protect what came out of a burning need from the homogenizing – though well meaning – forces of editors, marketers and publishers. Whether that will prove to be the book's charm or fatal flaw, time will tell. If it was to be released I needed to recognize it when I saw it. I've released too many records over the years that no longer resembled my songs. No more of that. I don't know what will come of this and outside of my own ego I kind of don't care. I'm just so grateful to have danced these steps with my creativity and with the idea of you, dear Reader. I'm so grateful for the gift this has been in my world. I do hope our paths happily cross down the road somewhere and that, perhaps, these musings will have lightened your load just a bit.

Certainty is a myth, friend. And this is such great news.

Be good to you.
Brian

CONTENTS

"On the off chance that you're not going to live forever, why not take a shot at being happy now?"

– Charlie Skinner (Sam Waterson),
The Newsroom written by Aaron Sorkin

Note to Self

I keep rewriting this book. I guess on account of how I keep rewriting my life or rather life keeps rewriting me. It's kind of hard to be clear on who's writing whom most days, you know?

Anyway, a rewrite or major edit sure beats the "tossing it entirely" I was tempted to do not long ago. Let me explain. I recently decided everything I've been writing and promoting in the world is fundamentally flawed. Yeah, so that day sucked. And then, as it is so fond of doing, it turned on me and gave me an unexpected gift but we'll get to all that later. Spoiler alert: it was the myth of certainty.

As I mentioned, I've wanted to write this book for some time now. My hang up has been what I'm writing will almost certainly fall into the category of self-help. Ugh. I don't want to tell you how to live your life. That's nonsense. That feels so arrogant and somehow ugly to me, despite the fact I love to read such books myself. You're the only one who knows what's right for you ultimately, as am I for me. Hold up. There's the ticket. I'm going to write this – whatever it is – to me. Not a past me but a future me who might need a refresher about how we (he and I) got here.

Maybe someone else will read these pages, maybe not. That's not the point. The point is that this is me writing to a future me and saying "Hey! Fella! Here's some things that work, some moments when you were onto something. Maybe try ________. Maybe that'll help." And just maybe it will.

On one of those decidedly not awesome days awhile back (you know the kind, right?), a dear friend of mine slapped me upside the head with a beautiful truth: I have a 100% success rate. Nothing I ever thought would break me has. Nothing. I'm still here growing, learning, and, yes, when I let myself see it, even thriving. Boom. But there are moments, days, heck, even years when that can feel hard to remember and believe. During those times the word "lost" doesn't come close to covering how I can feel. During those times it can be nearly impossible to remember and stay connected to the various teachings and tools that have often served me on the road to that 100% success rate. This book then is a letter to a future me who may be adrift in such an internal abyss. This is a letter to you. This is a letter to remind you of your own wisdom, tenacity, and beauty. You are a gift. Hopefully, there will be a few things in the pages ahead to remind and reconnect you with that truth. Onward.

Certainty is a myth. And this is such great news.

We're All Making This Up.

We're all making this up. Before we dig into uncertainty, let's just start here. We're all making this up. The so-called experts having been making up their specialty for a bit longer perhaps, but that's about practice, not pre-ordained knowledge. We're all making this up. Why start there? Why is the reality that we're all making this up so important? Critical even? Because it means we're all free to fail forward, as someone once said to me. It means ease up on you a bit already. More than that you're free to be liberated from the notion of failure at all. As am I, typing these words now, fighting the urge to be precious with them, resisting the thought there are right words and wrong words as I settle into these pages.

Unconvinced? Fair enough. I mean, that makes sense given the relationship between you and I is only a book cover and a few paragraphs long so far after all. There's a philosopher and writer – widely respected and revered for his insight into the human condition – named Ralph Waldo Emerson. He said,

> "Do not be too timid or squeamish in your actions. All life is an experiment. The more experiments you make, the better. What if they are a little coarse and you may get your coat soiled or torn? What if you do fail, and get fairly rolled in the dirt once

or twice? Up again, you shall never be so afraid of a tumble."

Here's my experience. Historically, I have wasted way too much time not taking action, believing people around me have better information than I do, I guess. Believing those who I admire, or revile for that matter, somehow have access to some kind of instruction manual. They don't. They just don't. Because we're all making this up.

Is that reality as liberating and terrifying for you as it is for me? To me it says with super high definition clarity, "Go! Do! Become!" Also, fall and get up and fall again. Do you know how to ride a bike? How did that happen? Training wheels? A push from Dad or Mom? A fair number of face plants? Of course. That's because, regardless of the experiences and knowledge of those around you, in order to ride a bike you have to find your center, your balance, your flow, in order to experience the exhilaration and freedom of the wind on your face as you race through the neighborhood.

It's not that there aren't experts or books to read or even things/people we consider authorities. I'm thinking here of teachers, doctors, lawyers, craftspeople, etc. I'm also thinking of textbooks, research journals, the Torah, the Bible, the Quran, etc. Those are all great resources, but the only leg up they have on you is someone else made them up before you arrived.

I'm serious about this by the way. Trace it back. Really. Any of the people you admire started at some point. They started. Period. They didn't step fully prepped and masterful into whatever it is you think they're awesome at. This is true for professions, for relationships, for whatever. Mastery is preceded by starting, always. It is that inherently simple and it is that inherently complex. Not the last time we'll bump into such an apparent paradox on this journey by the way. Before I leave this point and move on, let me try it from another angle.

My favorite class in high school was the one about managing my personal finances well. In college it was that class about finding the ideal life partner, building a lasting healthy relationship, and having amazing, playful, loving sex. Or that one that taught me how to pick a career at 21 that will be sustainable and fulfilling for a lifetime. You didn't take those classes? What?! Of course you didn't! Because we don't teach them! We don't teach people any of the things that later will be at the epicenter of what drives them and shapes their experience of life. We expect parents to do so, who were taught by parents, who were taught by…well, you get the idea. And then we look at each other through the lens of our own uncertain take on the world and either judge each other for not doing it right or assign a disproportionate level of credibility to someone or some group that seems confident they've figured it all out.

My point, whether you read another page of this book or not, is it's okay not to know. It is ok not to know.

A few years back I had the opportunity to see the Dalai Lama speak. He was doing a talk on creativity with actor and activist Richard Gere. Something happened at that talk that changed my world. Regardless of your religious affiliation or lack thereof, the Dalai Lama is clearly a well-respected and revered religious figure and authority. Agreed? Cool. Anyway, there were probably a few thousand folks packed into the theater where he was speaking on Emory University's campus in Atlanta. We were deep into the question and answer portion of the program.

I wish I could remember what the question was specifically, but I recall the audience member who had arisen to ask the question was asking one of those huge, meaning of life type questions. One of those questions we look to figures like the

Dalai Lama to answer, to give us certainty, something to hold onto in this perilous and often painful human experience.

I remember the question had the audience in rapt, pin drop quiet, attention. I remember the asking of it seemed to go on forever from the asker, through the translator, to the Dalai Lama nodding thoughtfully as we all sat breathless. I remember the question reaching its end, the translator translating the last few words, the Dalai Lama listening closely, cross-legged, wearing huge glasses and a visor against the stage lights. I remember him thoughtful and attentive taking in the last few words. I remember thinking – no, feeling – a great truth was about to be revealed, feeling this must've been what it was like to listen to MLK, or the Buddha or Jesus for that matter. Then he took a breath and answered in stilted English,

"I don't know."

The audience erupted in applause and laughter. I don't know what the experience of the moment was like in the minds of those around me. I'm sure some people found it just a light and comical moment and moved on. I'm sure some found it a disappointment. For me this answer erupted in my mind. For me this was as revolutionary a truth as Jesus declaring the highest, most transformative action is a loving one. Or the Buddha sharing all there really is, is now. Or Gandhi demonstrating that true change comes from being the change we wish to see. The Dalai Lama had just given us permission not to know! I don't have to have all the answers! Wow.

For me, after a lifetime of constantly striving above all to get it "right," this was a monumental weight lifted. This was nothing short of liberation. It is okay not to know. Ask questions for sure. Inquire. Explore. Dig deeper. And when you don't know? That's perfect too.

If you've picked up this book, which is, in part at least, about living a more fulfilling and meaningful life, then on some level you hunger for a more fulfilling and meaningful life. Or, you're a friend of mine and want to make sure I have money to buy food. In any event, I wanted to start our conversation and journey through these pages by saying two things that I know for sure:

1. It's 100% okay not to have the answers.
2. We are, all of us, making this up as we go.

Do you feel the significance and liberation of that? You get to strive, risk, and dare. You get to go boldly. In fact, that's precisely how it's done. There's a lovely quote said in several different ways by the author Ray Bradbury himself and others over the years. My favorite version comes from a New York Times piece,

> "If we listened to our intellect, we'd never have a love affair. We'd never have a friendship. We'd never go in business because we'd be cynical: 'It's gonna go wrong.' Or 'She's going to hurt me.' Or 'I had a couple of bad love affairs so therefore...'
>
> Well, that's nonsense. You're going to miss life. You've got to jump off cliffs all the time and build your wings on the way down."

How great is that? When I used a version of this quote for one of my "Hindsights" I added, "...because that's how it's done." (More on Hindsights later.)

We're all making this up.

There's another layer to this "I don't know" awesome-sauce. This layer is where it is really activated by the way. Since

I'm on a quote tear, what's one more? A smart person – I haven't been able to track down which one of you – but a smart person said,

> "True listening is the willingness to be changed."

Nice, right? See, in the wake of admitting you don't know something, life can get really scary. After all, uncertainty is not exactly the most prized of human experiences. In this case, though, uncertainty comes bearing gifts. This is where faith and openness take the stage with uncertainty and this is where magic can ensue. So, after you admit to not having all the answers (duh), open wide, listen closely, be willing to be changed. Messages will soon begin appearing if you're open and listening. Messages that come dressed like uncertainty but talking like answers. Give it a try. What's to lose? Later, we'll dig into some tools that can help you do this.

When I was first starting out as a singer/songwriter in New Orleans, one of the luminaries in the singer/songwriter community was a woman named Gina Forsyth. A few lines from one of her songs have stuck with me more than 20 years later and they are super relevant here:

> "Fall on your face / That's exactly what it's there for / Go on and make the same mistakes then go and make some new ones next time."

So, let's dig in shall we? If you're making this up and so am I, then let's start swapping notes. That's what this book is, assembled and written in the random and occasionally poetic way my mind works. In a way I'm increasingly daring to celebrate and embrace, and each time I do, I feel freer to boldly be me. Free to fly and fall and fly again. Free to jump off cliffs and build wings on the way down at every opportunity.

I'm not a PhD. I don't have a Master's degree. No hit record or bestselling book to allow you or I to point to as providing me some arbitrary, but mutually agreed upon, credibility. I'm just a guy on a journey like you, full of beauty and pain and often beauty in the pain. I'm just sharing what's working for me and what's not working for me in the belief when we set aside the need to be doing this life thing "right," when we splash more playfully around in the messiness of life, and when we share with one another the triumphs and tragedies that ensue, we give each other permission to leap, dare, crawl, play, embrace, fall, learn and love with all our might. We give each other permission to be who we most want to be, to live the lives we most want to live, to allow and celebrate that what that looks like will change radically over and over again throughout the course of our lives.

In the pages ahead, I'll be sharing stories, experiences, and truths I've stumbled and bumbled my way to on my journey so far. No "10 step" catch all answer, no one tool, and I'm sure, not without occasional (hopefully reinforcing) redundancy. Perhaps you'll find some tools that work for you. Perhaps, some things I've been through and/or learned will spark an entirely new lesson for you to live and share. In any event, my commitment to you is to leap off of as many cliffs as I can in the pages ahead. To give you as wide open and honest a view of my experiences as I can because, as a singer-songwriter and speaker I have learned repeatedly what is most personal to us is also often what proves to be what is most universal.

The author Elizabeth Gilbert was asked one thing she knows for sure. She characterized her reply as coming "in a bright instant, with absolutely no hesitation." She said,

"I did not come here to suffer."

Truth. Neither did you, kind reader. In case no one has told you and you've been waiting for permission, please allow me: You have suffered enough. You *have* suffered enough. Let's see if, together, connected through these words and pages, we can both live that permission. Let's see if we can, together, leap into the fullness of the lives we most want for our brief time here. Let's see if we can embrace that moving target as the beautiful, blissful, agonizing, poetic romp and tumble that it is. Agreed?

Thank you, in advance, for finding your way here and opening yourself to these words.

Oh, and one last thing, in the interest of full disclosure I should tell you something up front. I made all this up. Cheers.

Certainty is a myth. We're all making this up.

The Last Place

You know the cliché: "It's always the last place you look." Like most clichés, it is one because it's true. Happiness is like that in my experience. I look for it in a relationship, a job, money, where I live, where I travel, what I eat, drink, smoke, how I exercise, how I play. Of course, it's in none of those things. And it's in all those things. The trick is it's not "out there." It is 100% an inside job. Truly.

Remember that time you were running late and you couldn't find your keys? I mean you searched high and low. You were certain they were here and then there, then the other places. You got frustrated, cursed, stomped your feet, gave up, prayed to St. Anthony, sighed and hung your head. Then (cue choir of angels) they were right where you'd left them and something was on top of them covering them from view. Out the door you went.

Were the keys there the whole time? Yep. You probably even passed them or brushed up against them several times before you finally noticed them. The thing is that's ultimately what you did. You noticed them. You didn't discover them or create them or in some other way force them into existence. You simply noticed them. You became aware of them and in so doing they became "real" for you, and so you took them, walked out the door and onto your journey.

In my experience, happiness, contentment, or even just a deep cleansing breath, work just like that. It is here for me in this moment and, yes, in a relationship, a job, money, where I live, where I travel, what I eat, drink, smoke, how I exercise, how I play. But that is not because of the "doing" of any of those things. It is because I notice it's there. Right now. See, it *is* always the last place you look. Could it be all these externals are getting in the way of my experience of joy now?

Make no mistake, I'm not hating on drive or goals or ambition. Such things are deeply and beautifully engrained in the human experience. And, in my human experience, these can all be useful tools for finding the motivation to dig deeper into the juice of life. I think the essence of what I'm asking is this. Let's assume you set out after your goals, your dreams, in whatever area of your life, and you 100% "achieve" them. Yay! What next? No, seriously. What next? If that far-off goal is the driving force, the driving destination, then what happens after your arrival there? I ask because it seems we're always busy heading somewhere all the time. Well, what's the end? What's the target? I don't know that we have clearly set a target we can recognize as an arrival point, a point that calls for the cessation of all the incessant striving. This whole notion of focusing on who you will be and how great it will be once you get where you're going is true in all circumstances – including your faith – right? If you are going to church to find some sort of peace, then peace is the drive, the goal, isn't it? Striving, striving, striving.

My point is I have come to the conclusion I am often so busy striving that I'm blowing right past that which I seek. Far too often I catch myself burying my keys under piles of goals, piles of someday. Enough of that.

This is at the heart of the good news behind the reality that certainty is a myth.

Allow me to make my case...

Certainty is a myth. Isn't it great when you finally look in that last place?

The Myth of Certainty

My head is not my friend these days. I'm sitting here typing this drenched in beautiful sunshine. I can't feel it. This has been going on for a bit now. Yep, I'm obviously dealing with some degree of depression. I've been here before. It will lift. I remember a conversation with my ex-wife when we were frustrated my depression wouldn't budge. My comment was that while depression is, of course, a very real disease and something I live with and through, I think it's also worth entertaining the thought that sometimes I'm unhappy because I am, in fact, unhappy. That's where I find my life again at this moment. Ugh.

For me, it always seems to circle back to the same primary issue: my inability to convert the things I love to do, that I excel at, and are actual paid positions for some people, into actual sustainably paid positions for me. So, I end up perusing job boards that have nothing for me, networking in pursuit of jobs the notion of which scare me on a soul level, feeling ashamed I can't be normal like everyone else and just generally chasing my own tail and making myself progressively more unhappy. There must be another way. There just has to be. I'm increasingly inclined to think that way is to be happy, I mean to make happiness the priority, the choice I'm making, the means *and* the ends.

Certainty is a myth. All evidence in my life and all the lives I've ever encountered bear this out. There is no such thing as certainty. Everything changes. Money, jobs, relationships, governments, heck even mountains change. Think about this for a moment. Regardless of your age, is any aspect of your life exactly the same as it was ten years ago? I mean totally unchanged. How about five years ago? How about one year or even six months ago? I'm certain, if you honestly assess any aspect of your world, you'll find it has changed. That says to me, fundamentally, nothing lasts. Knowing nothing lasts says to me whatever pain I'm experiencing will shift. That also says to me whatever joy I'm experiencing – or fantasizing about and idealizing – will be equally transitory.

The more I embrace this reality the more it becomes the key I've been searching for. What key you ask? The key to this mystical place gurus, therapists, and self-help experts have been going on about for as long as I can remember. The key to being in the now. The key to being in the moment. If I know for sure everything is going to change, then I feel called to drink it in while it's here like lapping up cool water from a spring on a hot summer day. I'm under no illusion I'll be able to hold the water in my bare hands for long, but that doesn't stop me from happily scooping it up and splashing as much of it on my face, head, and shoulders as I can while I can. What if I applied that same playful approach to the features and moments – watershed or otherwise – of my life? Drinking them up while they're here. Knowing I cannot, and will not, possess them for long. Certainty is a myth and my grandmother has been right all my life when she has said over and again, "There's nothing so permanent as change."

Oh, one more thing on this point, I was recently chatting with my grandmother on the occasion of her 100th birthday celebration weekend. We talked about geopolitics and her recent deep interest in the future of our exploration of the universe, among other things. Yeah, I know, she's crazy smart and cool.

Anyway, as the conversation neared a conclusion, she shared with me how her understanding of the world has evolved past the "nothing so permanent as change" insight. She said she's become convinced the key then is to be in the moment, because it will not last and, perhaps more importantly, because this moment is all there is. Preach, Grammie, preach.

Certainty is a myth. Grammie was right all along.

Okay Then, What Next?

So, if I accept the premise that the notion that I'll arrive – or have arrived – at some fixed experience of life, that the notion of certainty itself is indeed a myth, what do I do with that? I'm convinced it's about showing up fully as who I believe I'd be in some longed for someday. Showing up as that person now. How does he walk, talk, think, eat, and/or play? What's his energy and way of engaging the world? I can do/be those things now. Why not? Won't that be more fun anyway? I'm not denying pragmatic limitations like perhaps I can't charter a plane to go off to some distant land at a moment's notice, but what is it I think I will get from that experience? What do I think it will feel like? Adventure? Spontaneity? Playful joy? Those feelings are something I can cultivate right now and aren't those feelings what I'm really after anyway? Equally if not more important is I can show up to the tough stuff, the really slippery painful stuff that will arise, from within the mindset and subsequent behavioral set I believe I'd possess in my fully actualized ideal life – that ideal someday.

Let me offer an example. This example happened in two steps, roughly one year apart and, poetically, both while working in retail. I'll explain and it's more entertaining and germane to our conversation here than you might think.

Before I do that, allow me an aside. You see I was about to go on at length about a time when I was looking for a professional level job when I thought, "What a condescending term that is now that I say it!" What I mean to say is I was looking for a job that would pay white-collar pay, that would be structured more like a… nope, still sounds awful. We'll get to the ah-ha's I promise, but first let's dig into what an arrogant, entitled punk I was thinking like just then.

Look, the fact is I'm a tall, lean white guy who was raised in various upper middle class tall, lean white guy communities. I was born into what amounts to the lottery jackpot of 20th century situations. I'm well educated – as I was always expected to be – and more or less constantly assured of a family safety net. I was not raised a 1%er but we were blessed to be up there somewhere. I've made choices in my life – my choices – that have me currently and, actually, for some time now in a precarious position in my financial/career circumstances. Make no mistake, however, I am fully aware these precarious circumstances are due to choices I've had the luxury of making. All that to say, it is clear to me right now I've been seeing the world through an unconsciously arrogant lens.

Obviously, implicit in framing my work in the section ahead is no small sense of seeing it as somehow beneath me. This is also true of the lens through which I've looked at many such jobs in the past. What a jerk move! While it's true I have other gifts and skills that may qualify me for other segments of the workforce we as a culture have decided to celebrate more and pay more, that does not make these jobs beneath me. It damn sure doesn't make the myriad of smart, hardworking people I've been honored to call colleague and friend in such jobs over the years beneath me. If anything, the converse is true. This kind of thinking is just another bastion, another foothold, of someday, destination, externals-that-promise-some-mirage-of-happiness thinking. It's another example of me buying into the dangerous and useless myth of certainty.

Anyway, I'm done with that arrogant (and ignorant) side of my head. I'm done with that kind of thinking that artificially and falsely elevates me and, in so doing, removes me from the moment, from the now, where my happiness is waiting. The truth I've come to learn by experience is there is no such thing as a job that is *beneath* me, though there are certainly ways I can show up to a job in a way that *is* beneath me. This notion that I "deserve" better inherently implies people in positions we all rely on, but would perhaps rather not do ourselves, are somehow less than. That's nonsense of course. Also, it misses the point about being the best me in the moment rather than defining myself exclusively by what I do.

Much like ambition and striving, I'm not hating on or denying the value of money and wanting to do things that make more of it. I will say, however, it's worth remembering we've all met or heard about plenty of rich folks who were miserable and poor folks who were happy, so perhaps the money and perceived prestige weren't the determining factors. There's an abundance of research on that to be sure, but doesn't your experience validate it in its own right?

Anyway, perhaps all that is useful to consider the next time you (or I) are checking out at the grocery store or deciding what to tip a server. Happily, allowing myself to be painfully honest with myself about my own assumptions and prejudices was ultimately hugely useful in teeing up some really good stuff. So, back to our regularly scheduled program…

I was about to share two transformative moments that found their way to me over the course of a year. Ah-ha number one started when a job hunt process that everyone warned me would take a while and be super challenging turned out to take a while and, in fact, be excruciatingly challenging. Go figure.

I had been given the opportunity to resign from a job I loved and into which I had poured way too much of myself such that it had become my whole world, my destination. (Do you see a theme emerging?) So, rounding the bend on six months after "resigning," cut off from my former life and a social network that no longer felt safe, living in my parents' house again at 42, just about out of money, and with no opportunity or job having surfaced at all, I hit the want ads with the bar set lower and lower, like do-over, on the floor, whoever will pay me lower.

So, I ended up back in retail. The folks who hired me were super kind, respectful, and open, but I'd soon learn that wasn't the way upper management behaved and I found I was smack dab in the middle of a fear based management approach – proven over and again to be profoundly ineffective in the modern workplace by the way. I had hoped to contribute fully but also to just do my eight and skate. Instead, it played out more like counting every one of the 480 minutes or more down each day. How had this happened, I wondered? I thought my life was so great! I thought I was on the fast track! I thought I was in the game at last! Now I couldn't even remember what the sidelines felt like.

I told a friend I was still in touch with it felt like working on the island of misfit toys. It seemed most of the people I worked with were in the same headspace I was. They had been on some shining "professional" track and then in some way or another the wheels came off and now here they were. As one of my new colleagues put it, "...this was the last branch I could grab before I'd have hit the ground." Yeah, like that.

The kicker in my head was I'm the motivational-speaker-positive-quotes-follow-your-dreams-leap-and-the-net-will-appear-all-is-well-and-abundant guy and all I could think was, frankly, THIS *cannot* be my life! Can it?! That's not true. All I could think was that everything I'd been writing, saying, singing, pushing, and believing is wrong. Fun stuff.

Which led to this. One afternoon I was sitting in my car on my lunch break and I was looking around. The thought occurred to me, within a mile of me there were likely enough retail stores to account for a couple thousand workers. Having found in my store that most of the folks I worked with were just like me, another thought found a foothold: what are the odds even 2% of those workers will ever come close to living their dreams? In my mind, it was abundantly clear that is never going to happen. So then, I've been working to succeed as a singer/songwriter, speaker, author, coach, etc. and meanwhile all that follow your dreams stuff I – and the rest of my field – are shilling is false? Worse yet, it's a falsehood that can ruin lives or at least cause people to waste them striving and reaching for something that may prove to be a mirage. What was the lesson though, I wondered? Don't follow your dreams whatever you do? That couldn't be it.

I counted my way through the minutes of several more days utterly defeated and consumed by a darkness I could not see lifting. I thought about the writers and speakers I've idolized, the musicians whose passionate advocacy for a more loving passionate life have defined my vision of my own life. I thought about the deeply spiritual calling I have felt my whole life to be part of spreading this message of lifting people up. I thought about my passion for theories of motivation and happiness. It felt like smoke and mirrors at best and willful deception at worst.

Then something shifted. It may be true that I can't teach people – or myself – to follow *and* achieve their dreams. I can't even make a strong case for doing so. I can, however, reframe the purpose of dreams. I can teach people to notice what they really want, what's behind the dream. I can teach people how to be happy. That is a truth that still stands. That is a truth I could stand before the thousands and millions just like me and say with confidence and passion.

Here's what I now think. Dreams don't mean what I thought they did. They don't play the role I thought they played. They, in and of themselves, aren't the point. There's another layer dreams are merely the vessel for. There's a layer we believe liberates us to begin behaving in a way that gives us the chance to feel something we truly want to feel.

I laughed out loud the day this shift started for me. I laughed at the notion of shifting into some version of the "don't follow your dreams" guy. I laughed until it wasn't funny anymore, until it was just obvious and true.

And then I forgot it completely.

I fell in love with a new mirage, tossed everything out the window to chase it like it was the messiah come to save me and promptly found myself in less than a year right back in the same hole hitting the want ads with the bar set lower and lower, like do-over, on the floor, whoever will pay me lower. Such is the human experience. Learn a lesson, blow past it, crash, get reintroduced to the same lesson, but go even deeper this time. Which brings me to ah-ha number two.

Back into retail I dove. Weary, desperate, dizzy and bitter. Yeah, I was super fun to be around. Again, this is not where I thought I'd be. Maybe you can relate to that? For me, I thought I'd be on a tour bus somewhere, or at least enjoying a solid coaching practice and speaking career or even in upper management in some groovy company. I mean these are all things I'm qualified to be doing. That is not where I am. Why tell you this? Because I have been blessed for some time now to not have achieved my full potential. No, you read that right. Start a business. Fail. Start a business. Fail. Take a day job. Rock it utterly, but still be shown the door. Along the way, "big break" after "big break" not resulting in any actual big break. All the while talking over and again about how you can follow your dreams, achieve your dreams. I'm not complaining here. All of this may well add up to the biggest blessings of my life. For real.

So, I arrived back in retail having launched another new business in which I was struggling to find footing. When I accepted the grossly underpaid position it was entirely out of last resort need. A couple of days into my tenure I was in the parking lot stretching and prepping to go in when the lesson of a year earlier and the new hypothesis rattling around my head resurfaced and sort of shook hands. Bing! Enter ah-ha moment number two (or "no duh" moment if you prefer). Here it is: I cannot work at building the life I want for myself outside of this job, building a creative career so deeply entrenched in the notion of tapping into one's own strength and wisdom, tapping into one's own happiness now if I'm going to be miserable and bitter here. Nope. Can't do that. I can't be thinking about, praying about, talking about those things out of one side of my mouth and out of the other go into work every day bitter and pissed off that I have to be there. That disconnect doesn't work. I have to show up fully. I have to find my happiness now, as in right now. And thus, my new job became my Master's Degree in Brian-ness. After all, that far off destination of wealth and success that looks so much like Eden is a myth anyway, right? Certainty is a myth. Except the certainty of uncertainty and the certainty I alone control what happens between my ears which, coincidently, is also the only conduit I (or you) possess for taking in and interpreting the world. Truly. And I'm 100% in charge of that real estate. Okay then. Happiness it is. But how?

Certainty is a myth. Happiness, however, just might be a choice.

Now As Then

Oh, and, by the way, I'm using the example of these work experiences but what we're really talking about here is anything you're framing or experiencing as a struggle in your world regardless of the context or setting. But you got that, right? Cool. Anyway, here's what's been working for me. There are two tools I use every day. The first I call "Now as Then."

I leave for work early. Which, at present, is at a shoe store by the way. I get to the vicinity of work early. I stretch. I read something meaningful and inspiring (Elizabeth Gilbert's "Big Magic" has been my jam lately). I pray prayers of openness, you know, the "open the eyes of my heart" variety. I sometimes listen to inspiring songs. In other words, I get my head straight. I get ready for today's "project" because, of course, this isn't my destination just my current project. Certainty is a myth. I remember, as my boo put it, this isn't forever and today I *get* to play with shoes for a few hours. That's pretty cool, right? Then I drive the last bit to work, park the car, and do my final act of personal revolution. I sing just under my breath all the way to the door, "I get to be love love love. I get to be gratitude. I get to be love love love. I get to be gratitude. I get to be love love love. I get to be gratitude. I get to be love. I get to be love. I get to be love." Then – just before I go in and no matter the weather – I turn my back to the store, take in something beautiful on the horizon (often turning my face to the sky) inhale deeply and exhale saying the words "thank you." Then I'm off to be love and gratitude and be happy playing with shoes for a bit. Boom. Look, I know all that is extraordinarily cheesy, but it helps me get my head in the right place. Now as then.

Does that last all day? Yes and no. The foundation is set for sure but of course there are moments when I have to change the frequency (more on that in a bit). Clearly, I would need more tools to get me – no, to thrive me – through my day. So I started thinking about some of my heroes. I started imagining as I went about my day, what would Dr. Wayne Dyer do? What would he do as he was walking these aisles? How would he interact with his colleagues? How would he interact with the product? How would he talk with the customers? How about Elizabeth Gilbert or Oprah or Bruce Springsteen or Garth Brooks or James Taylor? Those are just a few of the ones I use, you'll have your own of course but what would they do? I mean that literally. How would they think, breathe, walk, talk, behave? Would they be calm or edgy? Sulking or strutting? Hmmm. Well I can play with some of those things. I can play with them whenever I choose to. Now as then.

And then I started thinking, well if I can imagine my heroes showing up in these ways, how would *I* do it? If that big dream came true, if my ideal fantasy of my life was realized right now, how would I show up to this moment? How would I think, breathe, walk, talk, behave? And I suddenly found – and find, because it's something I do every day, it's a practice – I find I really change *physically*. I go from being sulky and closed off, to strident and open, breathing deep and sure. I change *mentally* as I think thoughts of gratitude and delight in what's in front of me in this moment knowing the moment will pass. And I change *emotionally* feeling less burdened by my present circumstance and, thusly, more present to the palette of experiences and sights it offers to grow me with. Now as then.

Reminding myself certainty is a myth, that this moment will pass, frees me to stay in it. Behaving now as I believe I will when all my dreams come true, gives me shades of the feeling of the experience of my dream life and my dream self now. How great is that? Plus, as I play make believe and deepen my belief in the inevitability of that someday, I'm paving the way, practicing to be ready for that life. Now as then. Now as then. Get it?

Certainty is a myth. Pretend you're amazing. You just might prove yourself right.

Turn the Other Cheek

aka Change the Frequency

Of course, since I'm not actually an animated Disney character, that doesn't always work and for sure it doesn't stop the inevitable experience of the heavy, hellish stuff life can bring. And you know that stuff is coming and usually when you least expect it. It's kind of like the "good" stuff that way, actually. So how do you deal with that? I have another tool I've been using. I call it "Turn the Other Cheek." It was inspired by my friend Rev. Richard Burdick, a minister and the spiritual leader of Unity North Atlanta Church, who was giving me his understanding of the passage in the bible advising one should turn the other cheek, presumably in the midst of conflict. If you're steeped in scripture – or averse to it – please stay with me because my intention here is not to have a theological discussion but rather to share a perspective that's serving me and might be useful to you too if contextualized to fit your own life. Anyway, Richard was saying he feels that passage is often misunderstood. It's not about turning the other cheek so you can be struck on the other cheek. It's about turning the other cheek so you can see things differently. You can't turn to offer the other cheek, the other side of your face, without changing your view. Literally. You can't turn the other cheek without seeing the world differently.

That got me thinking about the Greek stoic philosopher Epictetus whose core philosophy as I understand it was that we cannot control the external world. 100%. Period. Trying to control the externals is not your job. He's quoted as saying, "People are disturbed not by things, but by the views which they take of things." In other words, it's all about perspective. With Richard's wisdom and Epictetus' philosophy rattling around my brain, I started thinking about how to approach the heavy stuff a day in my not-so-dream-come-true life might bring. And that brought me to the gym. Yes, the gym.

In the gym, there's a basic apparatus I think most people are familiar with called the bench press. It's called this, I presume, because it is a bench upon which you lay and from that position press weights up and down above your chest. Aptly named. Let's say I've been doing a certain weight on the bench press for a while and I find I'm easily able to do a few sets of 8, 10, even 12 reps without breaking much of a sweat. So, I decide it's time to add some weight. How does that go down?

I add a good bit more weight to the bar, maybe call over the muscle-bound dude who seems to live at the gym to spot me (you know the one). I then lay down into position and begin. As soon as the weight is in the air, I'm having second thoughts. Once I lower it to my chest and start trying to press it upward again, I'm somewhere between panic and what in the world was I thinking?! Then it's up. And, astonishingly, I immediately go again. By the third rep I am done but muscle-bound guy ain't having it so, cursing, I squeeze out a fourth rep before racking the weight, giving the muscle-bound guy a very cool "Thanks brah" and sitting up with a groan to catch my breath.

Now, if this wasn't the gym but rather "real" life, what happens next? In real life when, let's say, I go from feeling like I'm on a professional or personal track and then it changes dramatically, I'm crushed and furious. In real life I'm all, "I can't believe it! Everything was working! Everything was going great! I was cranking out a few sets of 8, 10, even 12 reps. Now I've got all this extra weight and I can barely squeeze out 4?! Just when I thought my life was finally working it's all falling apart! Why doesn't anything ever work out?! I am the worst at life!"

But in the gym? In the gym, I squeeze out a fourth rep before racking the weight, giving the muscle-bound guy a very cool "Thanks brah" and sitting up with a groan to catch my breath. Then I take a sip of water, get up, shake it off, casually walk around a bit, maybe wander over to the mirrors – the big mirrors, of course. I take a sly look left and right before posing just a bit in the mirror and smiling as I think, "Ha! I think I'm a little bigger already! Now that's what I'm talking about!" Because in the gym when more weight gets added and you can't do as much with it, it's not a sign of weakness, it's a sign of strength. It means you were ready for more. It means you're getting stronger. It's good news. It means it's working. I'm getting bigger. Do you get it?

What if we turn the other cheek in our lives? What if when something happens you didn't see coming – that doesn't feel good – you reconnect with the truth of you? That you reconnect with the truth that you are mighty? What if you turned the other cheek to see that if you've been given more weight it must mean you're ready for more. It must mean you're getting stronger.

That's what I work to do every day as I face those ridiculously difficult moments that can arise – you know the ones – because Epictetus was right and Rev. Richard is right and Gym-Brian is right. If I just take a beat in those breathtaking moments of challenge to release the notion I can control the externals, to remember I *can* control my response to it, and to turn the other cheek, well then, I just might find myself posing in the mirror, psyched to have more weight, and fired up that I'm getting stronger. At least that's what's working for me.

Before I move on from this section let me put this last point one more way. It's a playful and simple tool my inspired friend Natina – whom I met in retail by the way – gave me. We would say it to each other as often as needed. It's this: "Change the frequency." Change the frequency. When I feel myself slipping from Now as Then into some dark inner spiral I say aloud, "Change the frequency." In other words, change the focus of your mind. And so it does. Little by little. Change the frequency. Also, I find it useful to jump up and down just a bit as I say it and to wiggle all my limbs, but that's just me.

Certainty is a myth. But I can show up now as then, turn the other cheek, and change the frequency whenever I want to. (Flex.)

Yeah, But

Oh hello there two least useful words in my vocabulary. There's a quote from an author named Richard Bach whose books were transformational in my early life that goes, "Argue for limitations and sure enough they're yours." The single biggest, most consistent and most insidious way I find I do this is with these two words: yeah, but. I might proclaim I am miserable in a job, relationship, state of health, living situation – honestly the circumstance is less than relevant – but when any well-meaning loved one suggests any alternative and I do mean *any* alternative, I am primed and ready with an arsenal of "yeah but" to make a powerful case for shutting that idea down and staying stuck. And it's certainly not just ideas loved ones propose. Let's say I decide I'm ready for a new job, for example. I know this means networking, reaching out to folks, and staying open to what's out there. But what I do is open my laptop, browse the jobsites, and one by one tick off all the reasons why every job available will never work. Ever been there? And it for sure is not limited to career stuff. It's this whole self-defeating, ripe with assumptions and future telling, internal storytelling nonsense I use to argue for staying precisely where I claim I no longer wish to be. Why do I do that?

I use these words for one reason, or at least to only one end. I use them to shut something down before it even has the chance to begin. You know the old cliché, "What you resist, persists"? Again, it's a cliché for a reason. I have lately been finding whenever I honestly look for and bring my awareness to anything I'm resisting whether slightly or powerfully, I stumble upon some vestige of attachment or destination thinking I'm being called to release in favor of openness, in favor of trusting faith, in favor of now.

My point is this, I think "yeah but-ing" can be used as a powerful tool. Once I've drawn my awareness to it, I think it is a call to pause and notice something. It may be I'm yeah but-ing because I'm blowing past my comfort zone. Sometimes, of course, that's a good thing, sometimes it's a great thing. However, sometimes I'm just not ready and my yeah but-ing is there to protect and/or prepare me. Or it may be I'm yeah but-ing because I'm starting a cycle I've been through before and my intuition is saying "Hold up. We've done this before and it didn't end well. Do you have a new approach in mind? If not, hit the brakes please." Well, thank you intuition! That's actually super helpful! And sometimes, all that yeah but-ing creates the opportunity to offer gratitude to such warning/doubting internal voices and choose to move forward bravely and boldly anyway. To my thinking, any endeavor undertaken with full self-awareness is a worthy one that will absolutely yield powerful dividends if I continue to apply my awareness. The pause created by "yeah but" opens the door to awareness.

So, "yeah but" can be friend or enemy. It can help me build on the best pieces of a new idea I really like or it can cause me to get mired in fear as I fall into the trap of being convinced I need to be sure I know the "ideal" solution before acting and that nothing short of the ideal will suffice. Like most tools, it's a gift if you use it right and a hazard if you don't.

Why bring this up now? Because you're reading a book that's going to offer a lot of opportunities to try new tools which means your brain is likely to generate a steady stream of "yeah but" moments. That's okay. It's just useful to be aware of, and awareness is a powerful tool. "Yeah but" your way through these pages if you'd like, but own it if you do. You're likely trying to tell yourself something important.

Certainty is a myth. Yeah, but that's great news, right?

A Word About a Word

Now that we've covered that, let's hit another sticky point: faith. Yep, I said it. There's an extremely gifted life coach I worked with years ago named Charly Borenstein-Regueira who once told me she will not work with someone who does not have faith in some kind of higher power. Hmmm, thought I at the time, that seems very limiting. Now I believe she had it nailed.

The thing is if you've found your way to this book you are no doubt feeling like your life can feel different than it does; like there's a deeper experience of, I don't know, I suppose happiness and meaning to be found. If you don't feel that way, this book won't help. In other words, and put simply, I can't help you to a deeper experience of the joy of life if you don't believe in something deeper. Make sense?

To be clear, I'm not talking about Jesus. I'm not talking about the Buddha or L. Ron Hubbard for that matter either. I'm not promoting any specific dogma. Yes, I may reference different religious and spiritual icons but that's just where I'm often coming from. It is my greatest desire that you and I both step into the fullest and deepest experience of ourselves and of this life that we can. That's what I'm promoting. That's what's better for all of us. What path you take – spiritually – to get there is of far less consequence to me.

I'm talking here about the difference between belief and faith. I don't care what you believe in. I do care where your faith is.

Awhile back I threw my back out, again. If you've had this experience, you know it is an insanely debilitating pain. I went from being a healthy, active man to being completely incapacitated in a matter of minutes. No fun at all.

I was in a meeting a few days later and a colleague was asking me how I was feeling. I was explaining I'd made a lot of progress. I mentioned I was playing both ends to the middle so to speak, going to my western medicine primary care doc for a check-up and medicine and also to a chiropractor for an adjustment. She said,

"I don't believe in chiropractors."

"Bad news," I said, "because they exist. What you mean is you don't put faith in chiropractors. That's a different thing."

I wasn't just trying to be a sarcastic, smart aleck, though clearly I was being that. This is a valuable point. Acknowledging something exists is one thing and it doesn't require I invest in it at all. Putting faith in something is a whole other ballgame. What I have faith in I lean on, listen to, and turn to for healing and guidance. What do you invest your faith in? We'll talk about this more as we continue, but it's important to get clear about this. As I recall the author Marianne Williamson putting it when I had the pleasure of seeing her speak several years back:

> "Some of you are thinking, 'I'm not so much about the faith piece.' Let's be very very clear. Every single person on this planet in every hour, in every minute, in every second, of every day, has faith. The only question – ever – is in what? Is your faith in

the disease or the cure? The lonely or the unity? The fear or the love?"

Where you are investing your faith, and with what degree of intentionality, is in my experience the single greatest tool you have for living the life you want. Where you're investing your faith is a choice you're making in this moment and in this moment and in this one and on and on. It is the story you are writing and, therefore, the story you are living.

One last thing about this in case you're still uncertain about how to recognize you have faith. I mean, you may be thinking, I'm not a "church person" and I don't consciously think about faith. So, what does it look like?

Earlier I mentioned I can't help you to a deeper experience of the joy of life if you don't believe in possibility of something deeper. Let's reframe a bit. Have you ever pulled over or stopped what you were doing to watch a sunset? A sunrise? A rainbow? Have you ever found yourself listening to a song and crying? Or dancing? And then listened to it again and again? That compulsion to drink in a sunset is an honoring of something deeper. Being moved to tears or dancing by a song is an honoring of something deeper. The acknowledgement of something deeper in life is what opens the door to accessing what you want your life to feel like. Those feelings help direct your attention to where you want to intentionally invest your faith. And living faith with intentionality is the lynch pin in building and embracing the life you truly want for yourself. Well done you. You have the building blocks already. And that's the word on that word. Can we continue our conversation without getting hung up on it? Cool.

Certainty is a myth. God knows.

Every No Is For Me

I grew up with a Dad whose "glass half full" approach in all things was like an affliction. It was also a gift, to be sure, but a little too much sometimes. And, of course, now I'm like that too. Now, however, much like the perspective shifting tool we talked about earlier I believe this tendency to perpetually look for the good news in any and all circumstances serves me quite well.

If certainty is a myth, then the bad stuff will pass. Yay! However, if certainty is a myth then so will the stuff that feels good. Boo. Subsequently, I feel called to deepen the glass half full approach. Here's where I've landed for the moment. I came to my new approach in another chat with my friend Natina one night at our retail gig. On a side note, chats in such environments are hilarious because you're living in a fishbowl under constant surveillance so you talk in passing, straightening things as you do and in like 30 second increments. Anyway, Natina asked me how I handle no's. I knew she meant in regards to the rewards program we're required to pitch to customers for which we get dinged for any missed signups and to which customers often respond with dehumanizing rudeness. (Public Service Announcement: I don't care how many emails you get. Don't be a jerk to the counter-workers; they're just doing their jobs. Be nice or do your shopping online. End of PSA.) That's what she was asking about. But what fun would it be to answer that question?

I immediately dove down the rabbit hole and told her I'd get back to her. At the end of the night I told her I had an answer: Every no is for me. My faith teaches me the Universe wants me to prosper, that when I prosper, the Universe is prospered. If I believe that… Actually, let's not just blow past that. You may have had a "yeah but" just then. I'm saying the Universe wants you to prosper, benefits from your prosperity. Why not believe that? What value would believing the opposite add to my world and my relationship with life? Put another way (as recently arose in conversation with my best friend), the Universe is tired of reruns. The Universe has watched this episode where you struggle and suffer and paint yourself the victim over and again along with you. The Universe, God, is ready for a new more radiant, joyful and prosperous episode of you when you are. Perspective.

So, my faith teaches me the Universe wants me to prosper, when I prosper the Universe is prospered. Great. If that's true, then obviously every yes in life is "for" me and not "at" or against me. However, it follows if that's true then every no must also be "for" me and not "at" or against me. There must be some gift in that no just as there is in the yes. Just because the no is uncomfortable doesn't render the gift it carries as diminished or invalid. At the very least there's information in the contrast between how I'd like to be feeling and the discomfort of what/how I am feeling. Once again, it's perspective and, once again, that perspective is my choice. I'm using my mind to feel victimized by rejection, why not use my mind to feel elevated by it? Why not embrace the no's I receive with the same vigor, joy, and passion as I do the yesses.

Certainty is a myth. The gift of no's is not.

Words Matter

It is popular in our culture to share quotes and positive thoughts over the various social media avenues. It is equally popular to dismiss or even mock such positivity and hopefulness as lacking any substantive value. I mention that here to make a point. Obviously, much of what I'm describing as being useful tools on my journey thus far involve shifting my perception by changing my thoughts, awareness, words, and, subsequently, actions. This is exactly the kind of thing that can easily be dismissed by the roll-up-your-sleeves-pull-yourself-up-by-your-boot-straps-eat-your-meat-and-quit-talking-about-feelings crowd, right? The same crowd – or voice in your head – who will happily scream their heads off watching their favorite sports team play. Well, let's look at that.

The Super Bowl. For better or for worse, at this stage of our cultural evolution, athletes make bank. I mean exponentially more than teachers, for instance. So, since they're rich – because of us by the way – they must be taken seriously, right? I mean that's how we roll in the United States. You're rich. You must be very pragmatic, no nonsense, strategic and logical. Okay then. Back to the Super Bowl. Before the game in the locker room. Do they talk all logic, shake hands, and quietly take to the field? No. What is it these great athletes – the envy of our society – do before and as they take to the field? They chant, sing, stomp, jump, shout – mostly together to boot! They get their heads in the right space. They know what they need to feel like in their minds and bodies to be successful and they fake it, seduce it, coax, sing it, and/or jump it into existence. And we love it! I'm just saying, why would that not be true in other areas of your life?

Think about the pre-work practice I talked about earlier. The meditating, praying, and singing I do. It's the same practice as the pre-game practice. It's the identification of what mindset would best serve me in a given situation and choosing the thoughts and words that might best support that mindset. Make sense? You know the experience of not having the right mindset in a situation and how it can wreck a moment. Why not be intentional and empowered in choosing the thoughts, words, or even way of moving as you prepare for whatever you're preparing for? I'll bet you already instinctively do this before a date, job interview, big conversation, or even going into the gym. You set the tone with something you do, read, listen to, or think. That's all we're talking about here. Claiming your power and using it intentionally. It may not take away the nerves and discomfort in the moment, but it will make you ready for them.

Certainty is a myth. Words matter and can make all the difference. Go team!

Between Your Ears

Before we leave the topic of the value of words, let me drill down on something I touched on earlier but in a slightly different direction. Reality check. You control only one thing in life, truly. There is only one thing in all the universe over which you have exclusive purview. That's the bad news. The good news is it lives between your ears and it is also the only lens through which you experience and understand the world and your life. Seriously, that's it. The world, and your life, doesn't exist outside of your head. At least not in any way that has value or meaning to you. This is a heavy responsibility but also a golden opportunity.

There is a story factory in my head that would put the busiest Hollywood writing staff to shame. That factory is churning out stories every waking minute of my day. These stories draw off of so-called "facts" as I currently believe them, past experiences, doubts, fears, dreams, hopes, pain, pleasure, and on and on. The point is these stories I create in my head are the stories I live in my life. Again, I point to the experience of watching two people in the same circumstance – let's say socioeconomic status – approach it with vastly different attitudes and, therefore, have vastly different experiences. What's the difference? The story they tell themselves, and others, about themselves. Where's the story created? Between their ears.

You are a masterful storyteller so why not begin the practice of telling – and living – the best possible story for the experience of life that you desire for you? It will take practice. In my experience, starting a new habit – whether a new diet or a new way of thinking/seeing a situation – is no easy thing. In the next two sections, allow me to offer a couple of tools that serve me well in my writer's room.

Certainty is a myth. However, you're wicked strong right between your ears.

What Is Also True?

Rewriting a script I've been living is no easy task. If you've ever tried to change a habit or start a new one, then you know. It's often a series of advances and retreats. Backsliding will happen, and my mind will make an extremely compelling case why I would be better off staying where I am and not changing at all. What to do then? Well, the second tool I'll share with you will be about practicing the new thought pattern, the new belief about you and your life you'd like to see realized. This first tool, however, is all about convincing your mind to allow you the space to embark upon that journey to begin with.

It's the simplest tool, really. It's just a question. When you find yourself in a situation where you're slipping into a way of seeing your world you'd like to step free of, ask yourself what is also true? What is also true? When I was training to be a life coach, this was one of the "powerful questions" they drilled into our heads. Now I use it nearly every day. The power of it for me seems to be in how it honors the argument, if you will, my current way of thinking is making, while creating space for a new one. It's saying in my own mind, "Okay, I hear you and I can see that, but what else is true here?" Put another way, it's about asking what might I be ignoring or dismissing in this moment? And what new directions might be revealed if I shifted my attention to that piece of the puzzle?

There's an exercise I learned somewhere along the way that illustrates this point nicely. Pick a color. Let's say green. Now look around whatever space you're in right now. Notice only the green. Any shade of green you see. Ignore everything that is not green. Notice it in details and broad strokes. Just see the green. Go ahead, I'll wait. Good. Now look for blue. Just shades of blue. See only the blue. Perfect. Pick a third color of your choosing and look for only that. Well done. Did you notice what happens there? Each color is there all the time but the one you focus on becomes, well, your focus. Suddenly that color pops in the space. What you focus on grows. It's not unlike the experience of putting on a coat or a pair of pants you haven't worn in a while and finding a $20 bill in the pocket. I get so excited! It's like it was just given to me out of the blue. Of course, it was there the whole time, I just now directed my attention to it.

You can use this in the writer's room in your head. For me, it's about practicing two things. First, a willingness to notice when I'm bumping into thoughts that aren't serving me or in which I'm stuck (e.g., regarding a colleague, a dream, a relationship, health). And second, taking the time to ask myself what is also true here so I can shift my attention to some new perspective of the situation that does serve me. And I can do so right now.

Certainty is a myth. What is also true is I get to choose the colors I paint my mind with.

Hindsight

(No, not the 20/20 kind.)

The second tool I'll share with you will be about practicing the new thought pattern, the new belief about you and your life you'd like to see realized.

I write on the back of my car. On the rear windshield, actually. In life, among other things, I am a songwriter/singer, speaker, coach, storyteller, and author. But in recent years I've often been better known as that guy who writes on the back of his car. This may seem to be an odd tool, actually more like just an odd thing to do, but it is a powerful one for me when I catch myself needing to shift an element of the story I keep writing and rewriting in my head.

How I came to be doing this is a bit of a long story, but it's one of my favorites. It started with the Saints. The New Orleans Saints, of course. More specifically it started with their amazing, magical Super Bowl run in the 2009 season. I am a born-again New Orleanian. To be fair, I was reluctant at first, and by at first, I mean for years. Nevertheless, I moved there in the fall of 1990 to attend Loyola University and (with a couple of attempts to emigrate elsewhere) stayed until the great divorce of 2009, but that's not this story. Along the way, through the eyes and kind tutelage of my ex-wife and amazing friends, I flat out fell in love with the great, soulful Nation of New Orleans. Hence the post-Katrina ink I now bear evermore on my forearm making our blood relationship official. Anyway, I promised to explain the Hindsight thing so let's get back to it.

New Orleans, while a great city, is also a small town. So in the fall, during the great divorce of 2009, I had retreated to Atlanta seeking shelter with family and giving my ex and I much needed space to heal and rebuild without constantly crossing lives. That also happened to be the year when the Saints, having committed themselves to bearing the weight of being the symbolic epicenter of the rebirth of New Orleans, proved it to the rest of the world by making an improbable Super Bowl run.

Somewhere I have a picture I took on Bourbon Street after we won. It's blurry with emotion and movement, but it's of someone holding up a sign that reads, "Hell Just Froze Over!" Yeah, it was that improbable. Anyway…

I was convalescing post-separation/mid-divorce in Atlanta, feeling like a man without a country. I kept my connection to New Orleans, and a bit of a sense of who I was, through the TV screen and a rotating lineup of eleven men doing something previously believed impossible.

When we made it to the NFC championship, I'd stood all I could stand and I headed back home to watch the game in the French Quarter with friends. After that ridiculously amazing night – another story for another time – I headed back to Atlanta. On the way into town I stopped by my brother's place. I asked him to take off from work so we could go to New Orleans together to watch the Super Bowl from the Quarter. Happily, he did and so we did.

I drove a beat up 1996 Honda Accord at the time that made an awful buzzing sound every time you unlocked or locked it. I got an idea and stopped by an office supply store and found one of those window markers folks use when selling a car or getting married or whatever.

I remember it being freezing in Atlanta at the time but I gleefully circled my car marking the windows with Saints messages: "Honk if you're a WHO DAT! Geaux Saints!" "Black & Gold Super Bowl!" and, my favorite, "Finish Strong!"

My Falcons-fan (Bills first, Falcons second) brother and I piled into the car and headed off to New Orleans. Along the way, we were inundated with honking and waving. It was so fun! So connecting.

Fast forward a week or so and I'm continuing to receive smiles, waves, and (mostly) happy honks from folks all around Atlanta as I now sport my victory message. Then came a moment of epiphany. Out loud to myself in the car after one such encounter I said, "This is so fun! I wish I could do this all the time. Wait! I could do this all the time!"

And that's how it started, simply and happily because it was fun. Eventually I started calling them Hindsights. Now I do a new one more or less every week. Sometimes I make them up. Sometimes I quote directly or adapt a quote. Sometimes they're a commentary on something we're all going through like when I put up "Carpe Diem. Please." after Robin Williams' death. Sometimes they are a message directed at a friend who's going through something challenging.

More often than not, however, I write something I feel like I want/need to be reminded of as often as possible over the next week or so. I do it to rewrite a story I'm working on changing in my head, or to reinforce one. My experience as a writer and performer has taught me the more personal and truly vulnerable I am willing to be the more universal it seems to become. Certainly, the Hindsight bears that truth out week in and week out. Over the last year, that notion has been deeply reinforced through others' experiences as well as I've begun coaching people to their own insights and then enshrining them as Hindsights on their cars.

For me, this practice is not about putting a positive saying on the car and into the world, though that certainly is a happy side effect. For me, it's the practice of creating a quiet space to listen to myself, to listen to what the yearnings of my head and heart are at that moment. More often than not the best measuring tool is to ask myself what I've been longing to hear, something that if someone said it to me regularly would consistently keep the train on the tracks. When I find the most authentic tones there I always – always – have some emotional and physical response to that discovery. Sometimes it's joyful, sometimes tearful but always cathartic and liberating. I often describe it in other areas of my life as the "lift" – that feeling of lightness and expansion, of resonance when I know something is true for me, when I *know* it is the right choice for me. Do you know that feeling? Anyway, I then talk myself through that "thing" until I stumble upon some memorable way of expressing it that might fit on the rear windshield.

Oh, and here's something fun I learned during that New Orleans trip. If you were sitting inside my car and turned to look at the Hindsight it would obviously be backwards, right? However, when I look in the rearview mirror, tada!, it reads forwards for me. Nice, right? Also, the reason for the name Hindsight.

The point is, while asking "What is also true?" is a great tool for shifting my attention away from a thought pattern that no longer serves me and into a new perspective on something I want to change, setting up shop in the new perspective/story about the situation takes practice. For me things like the Hindsight are useful because they serve as randomized reminders to actively practice a new thought that *does* serve what I want. It allows me to gradually make that the new zero state in my thinking about something. There are other ways besides writing on your car, of course. Heck, there are apps you can use. My experience is the simpler the better. Also, like my rearview mirror that I don't know for sure when I'll look at next, the more likely that you'll randomly notice it and not have it just become a rote part of your space the better.

A final aside about the Hindsight experience, and what takes my breath away, is the unintended consequence of how impactful the Hindsights have been for others. I have lived a life rich with amazing experiences thus far. I have been blessed to publish one other book, more than a dozen records, and have spent much of my adult life touring the country serving as a singer/songwriter and speaker for audiences small and large, at holes in the wall and epically legendary venues. Yet, in my estimation, nothing I have ever done has had the consistent and wide-reaching impact the Hindsight has. I mean, it's a simple quote on my rear windshield that takes all of five minutes a week with a $5 paint marker. But it changes lives. I know it does because people tell me so. People write to me, follow the various social feeds, like/comment/share, honk, wave, smile and, yes, sometimes glare a bit. Impacted all.

Most poignantly for me personally has been when people stop me in parking lots or pull over to talk with me. Like awhile back, coming out of my day job at the time. It was cold and getting dark. I was loading up my stuff when a beat up "Sanford and Son" looking pickup truck that seemed to remember predominately being red at one point pulled up beside me. I love the city and its wide mix of people. Also, I've lived in the city enough and traveled enough to know when to bring a little (to put it nicely) "don't mess with me" attitude. Anyway, the driver, a rather gruff and grubby gentleman leans over and hollers to me through the passenger window:

"Hey!"

"'Sup," I said stiffly and with as much intimidating toughness as I could manage.

"I wanted to thank you," he said extending a calloused and weathered hand for me to shake, "I make it a point to drive down this street every day to see what the new quote will be on the back of your car. It makes my week. I look forward to it."

"Thank you," I said, utterly blown away.

This has happened many times. One evening a guy stopped me, saying:

"Do you know whose car that is?"

"Yes sir. It's mine."

Welling up with tears he said, "I love you man. Your words have been huge for me. You've gotten me through the day many, many times. Thank you."

"Thank you!" Who do you think was welling up then?

I'm not telling you all this to toot my own horn. I'm telling you because there's a lesson, a huge lesson.

So many great teachers, when talking about how to live the life you're longing to and have the impact you most desire, say essentially the same thing. Do what you can, with what you have, from where you are. It's a simple idea, but not a small one. Do what you can, with what you have, from where you are.

Too many times, I've been guilty of inaction awaiting the perfect plan. Trying to come up with the BIG idea. All the while I'm burning and yearning with a desire to be making a difference, to be living a difference. Instead I wait and plan and dream and bemoan I can't seem to get picked for the team and put in the game. What the Hindsight has shown me time and again is the profound truth of the power of doing what you can, with what you've got, from where you are. For me in this case, it's five minutes a week with a $5 pen I replace a few times a year. And it's arguably the most impactful thing I've ever done. Do you have that kind of time? Do you have that kind of money? I wonder what your "thing" could be or already is? Get it? Good. Then get it. Whatever "it" is for you. Go do it. Start today.

You don't become a marathon runner by running 10 miles on your first run ever. You don't lose 100 pounds in your first day of a new diet. You don't become a novelist in one sitting. You don't find your perfect mate by waiting until you're perfectly ready and making one call. You begin. You do what you can, with what you have, from where you are. You start by starting. You begin by beginning.

And you don't settle into a next new story all at once either. You recognize you're ready for a new one. You ask what is also true to see what "colors" you may have been missing but are available to you. And you begin to practice the new language of your new story by whatever means work for you. The sillier the method the better in my opinion.

Certainty is a myth. But you get to write the story as you go.

Amazingly, I have a few pictures of the very first Hindsight – and that's my brother Sean by the way. The one with the rear-view mirror is literally the moment I realized there might be something more here than just a Super Bowl celebration:

And here are a few examples of the Hindsights since then:

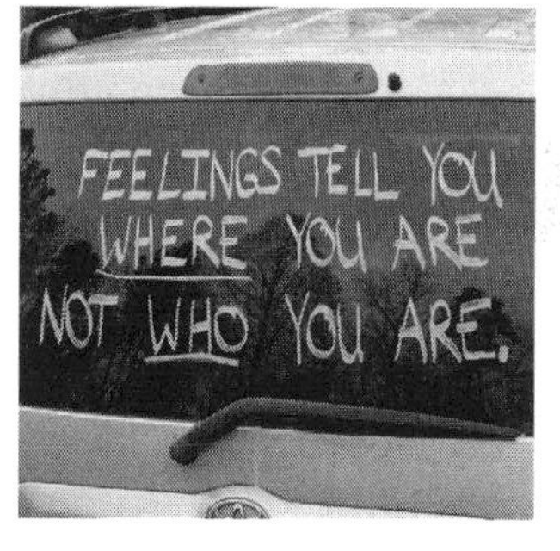

Owning Your Power

There's a trick to everything I'm talking about here, to everything I'm working on and through. In the end, it's about disabusing myself, not just of the myth of certainty, but of the myth I am powerless as well. My life isn't happening to me, it's happening through me. The more I own that, the less I play the victim and the sweeter the ride.

Take the practice of gratitude, for instance, which has been en vogue in pop-psychology circles for some time now. When I practice gratitude – which is to say when I direct my attention to that for which I am grateful in my life or in a moment or experience – I'm not physically changing the environment I'm in of course. I am, however, claiming my power and ability to interpret and respond to that environment as I choose, in a way that best supports the story I choose to be living in that moment.

Talk about changing the frequency by the way! Gratitude regularly rocks my world with this. There are days, you know like yesterday (seriously), when I'm fighting anxiety and all the darkest and most cynical internal voices so I shift to practicing gratitude. Does it feel dumb and forced at first? Of course it does! But, wow, can it shift my world! Learning new things always feels awkward at first. That's what change feels like. Also, have you ever exercised when you didn't feel like it? But you were super glad you did afterwards? Right. Change can feel like that too. My go-to these days when I feel like I'm starting from the bottom is to, well, start from the bottom; to get back to basics. Let's say a customer comes up to the counter at the store. I ask them how they are and, politely, they reciprocate asking me the same. My sincere response on such days? "I woke up this morning, so, you know, that's pretty cool!" Inevitably we both laugh, express some degree of amen-ness together, and the energy lifts. Every time. Gratitude. Boom.

I know in many ways these things are redundant. That's good news. Expressing what's true from many angles doesn't diminish its value, it deepens our understanding of its richness. In this case, the richness lies in the sheer immensity of power you possess in every moment to radically shift your experience of your life with utter simplicity and relative ease. Like by practicing gratitude.

Certainty is a myth. You are mighty. Repeat after me: "I woke up like this."

Change the Frequency

How am I doing so far? Good? Maybe it's time for a "change the frequency" break. Let's give that a little practice. It's useful not only when you're in a negative headspace but also when you're deep into a positive one but needing to refresh your attention. So, stand up, stretch, shake from head to toe like a dog fresh from a swim, bounce up and down a bit and say – in as fun and silly a voice as you can – "change the frequency" three times. Deep breath. Okay. Onward.

Certainty is a myth. Change the frequency often to stay tuned into that truth.

Deify Less, Glorify More

And while we're on the topic of your awesomeness let's talk about how we lose touch with that truth. Let's talk about deifying. You know this term, right? To deify is to make a god of. We, as a culture, are huge fans of doing this. We do it with artists, athletes, actors – mostly "a" words it seems. No, seriously. Whether it's Oprah, Dr. Martin Luther King, Brad Pitt, Beyoncé, or whoever, we deify the crud out of people. I'm all for celebrating someone's gifts and the beautiful ways they contribute to the world. The trouble is we tend to elevate them as somehow being more than human. The problem with that is it's a copout. It's a way of shirking responsibility for our own gifts, for our own greatness. Oprah? Oh, she's special I can't do that. Dr. King? Oh no, he had a special gift I can't do that. Jesus? Well, maybe we'll steer clear of that one but you get the point, right?

If I can dial up and lock my thinking into the notion that those who I admire were anointed in some special way, then I can let myself off the hook for not living up to my own brand of greatness. I create a rational basis for staying within my fear and comfort zone. I'm not saying we should all strive to be Oprah. I'm saying, as it has often been said, we all have some unique brand of "music" within us. I'm saying your "music" ought to be shared with the world. And I'm saying all the people you admire are just that, people. So, what do you do with that? Deify less, glorify more.

Allow your heroes to have flaws, even big ones. Notice them. Honor them. Then choose to glorify how beautiful it is that they don't dwell in those flaws, they use them as fuel, they still show up fully to their gifts and share them with the world. I find when I allow for that, celebrate, even glorify that, that doing so somehow sends a message to my own internal headquarters. It sends the message that I don't need to be perfect to contribute. I don't need to be perfect to share my "music" with the world. What's more I can embrace – heck, even be entertained by – my own imperfections. They don't diminish what I have to offer the world. For all I know, they enhance it. Just look at my heroes. Make sense?

Deifying less does not diminish anyone's contributions. It does, however, liberate us all to make our own. It liberates us to look to each other as mirrors of magnificence, empowering each other to be more of who we truly are. Less deifying, more glorifying the beautiful, perfect mess that is each of us. That'll do. Oh, and, no dying with your music in you, ok?

Certainty is a myth. Deifying less elevates us all.

Insides Out

No, that wasn't a typo in an attempt to reference the Oscar winning Pixar film, although that's actually a great stepping off point. When a movie like that, digging into the inner workings of the mind in all its majesty and mess, is so universally well received there's a really important lesson. Again, we're all going through this together and we're all making this up as we go.

So, insides out. For the most part, I'm a fan of the advent of social media. It gives me a chance to be in greater touch with people I care about and likely would have lost touch with otherwise. It also gives me exposure to lots of things I wouldn't otherwise seek out or see, and some I wish I could unsee. It's much like TV in that way, actually. And just like TV it's important for me to remember I have a remote control, so to speak, and I can change the channel, turn it off, or even just unplug the darn thing if I need to. To my thinking, the single biggest pitfall in social media is it makes it far too easy to get in the habit of comparing my insides to other people's outsides. This is not good. This is not useful. This is just plain destructive sometimes. And I'll bet you know exactly what I'm talking about.

I have asthma. I've had it all my life. Sometimes people ask me what it's like to have asthma to which I usually reply I don't know because I don't know what it's like *not* to have asthma. This is my zero state. It doesn't hamper or impact my life really. It's just what living my life looks like. I have maintenance tools I use and when I don't it can lead to problems. But that's true for plenty of folks without asthma. I don't just manage my asthma; I thrive through it. Heck, I even ran a marathon. I'm also a published author with attention deficit disorder and a motivational speaker who lives with depression and anxiety and a creative introvert who excels as a performer. So what? The problem when I start comparing my insides – and my labels – with other people's happy photos and latest accomplishments is I forget they've got their own cast of characters prattling on in their own head with their own labels and growth opportunities they're struggling with. The problem when I compare my insides to other people's outsides is I can forget my own mightiness, that *you* might forget *your* own mightiness. That won't do. It's actually feeling increasingly like my life's work is to make sure you don't forget. Yes, you.

The point here is not to scold you or add to your to-do list by creating another bunch of exercises to help you shift your experience of your life. The point is, again, to draw your attention to the simple fact that you're already making a choice of how to experience it. If it feels heavy, why not choose again? You're already in the moment of choice so it's not out of your way. Why not let your friends be themselves, living their own life, having their own journey – seen and unseen – which is not the same as your journey? Maybe next time you're browsing your favorite social media feed and you feel tempted to do that heavy comparison nonsense, instead, say to your screen (preferably out loud), "Well done friend. We rock, don't we?! How mighty are we?!" 'Cause we are. All of us.

Certainty is a myth. The fact we're all the heroes of our own stories is not.

Do Anything

You know what I love? Being overwhelmed. Okay, I don't actually love being overwhelmed. What I love is there is inevitably a moment when I become aware I am, in fact, overwhelmed. Often times this moment coincides with a venting session with a friend as I bemoan my state of overwhelmed. By the way, this isn't just about task oriented stuff. I'm also talking about being overwhelmed by life, by career, relationship, by any future stuff. You know that feeling, right? So, there's that moment when I'm poised to tear out the little hair remaining on my head and suddenly I see there's a gift. If I'm overwhelmed and feeling like everything needs to be on the top of my to-do list, then doing anything is progress. Anything I do is a win. How great is that? I know that seems overly simplistic but, like the certainty myth, just look at it in your life. The notion that certainty is a myth is an easy conclusion to reach when you realize nothing in your life has stayed the same indefinitely. The notion that in the midst of feeling overwhelmed by the shear endless volume of life's to-do lists there is a liberation in knowing that this means any action is progress, that doing anything moves the needle, is equally self-evident. Cool, right?

Let's not bounce from here without touching on a trickier side of being overwhelmed. Energetically this is useful as well. What I mean is, when you are overwhelmed about more metaphysical things you can't seem to see any tangible action steps you can take at all. Perhaps you just know you want something to change. Honoring that simple intuitive need, offering that up to whomever you prayerfully offer things up to, is enough. That's doing anything and, therefore, making progress. The author and teacher Mike Dooley puts it perfectly when he writes, "When you don't know what you want, want happiness, and when you just don't know what to do, do anything. Go."

What he said.

Certainty is a myth. Feeling overwhelmed blows. So, I do anything and – boom – all I do is win.

Do Nothing

Now, having said all that. If you're not sure what to do next, sometimes the best thing to do is nothing. Over the last week or so I've had a couple of my best friends decide to just take time to do nothing, to unplug, to follow their heart's every whim and desire. The result? They are marveling at how much lighter, more focused, and more peaceful they now feel. Well, isn't that interesting?

I've had the great honor over the years of being a part of the planning and leading of retreats and camp/conferences. It occurs to me as an adult that many people – myself included – spend or long to be able to spend vast sums of money and travel long distances to participate in such experiences. Don't get me wrong. I'm a big fan and I toy with the notion of opening my own retreat center someday. The thing is, what is it I think I will get out of going away on retreat and how do I think it will happen once I get there? What's the goal? Well, it's probably to feel lighter, more focused, and more peaceful than I feel now and subsequently to have the sense of being more happy. How is this accomplished? I'm glad you asked. In my experience, much of the magic of retreats is accomplished by creating space for fully volitional action, quiet, and perhaps rest. Well, dear Brian (and dear Reader), has it not occurred to you that you have all those tools right this moment? I can accomplish that goal, sate that need, by simply stocking up on some groceries, turning off all of the electronic things, and locking the door at the start of a weekend. I can do that now, whatever I need a retreat to look like. Maybe it's less yoga and a bit more local parks (and perhaps a dash of Netflix). Who cares? Stillness, quiet, simply being with my breath and thoughts is free and available to me right now. Or, if I want to splurge, it's at least just an affordable and groovy Airbnb away, right?

Point is if you're feeling overwhelmed, lost, or just plain "off" maybe consider taking some time to just do nothing. You're welcome, by the way.

Certainty is a myth. Feeling overwhelmed blows. Doing nothing doesn't suck at all.

You Don't Need a Plan

Ok, so of course having a plan can be useful. What I mean is it seems very clear to me at this point that all the goals, dreams, or even just stuff I've ever been after aren't what I've actually been after. In the end, what I truly want is whatever I think it will *feel* like to have, do, or achieve whatever the object of my desire is. It's the feeling. As I alluded to earlier, the problem is we as a people seem to have a complicated relationship with feelings. In so many ways, we seem to value feelings and passions deeply. Yet we also seem to very easily dismiss them as not being pragmatic enough and even as a sign of weakness. For instance, in business circles we have a way of diminishing the value of things like emotional intelligence to the point of irrelevant – or certainly less than – by labeling them "soft skills."

My sense is, in many fundamental ways, this gets back to a desire to cling to the myth of certainty. Feelings tend to come and go with what can at times be a dizzying level of speed and unpredictability. This is not comfortable. However, as I hope it's beginning to be clear, discomfort is not the enemy of alignment, progress or even happiness. What's more, the more I embrace life's apparent fluidity, aka uncertainty, the more I can show up fully to whatever I'm feeling, knowing for sure it will pass and it has value. As I wrote in a Hindsight awhile back, feelings tell you where you are not who you are. I digress again. Squirrel! Back to feelings and plans.

Why do I love my spouse, my car, my job, my music? I love them because of how each of them makes me feel. They don't have inherent, intrinsic value. They really don't. Their value is almost entirely derived from how they feel to me. This is not to diminish the parts of our lives, and ourselves, we hold dearest. The reason recognizing where their value actually comes from is important is that we often approach their pursuit backwards. We try to *think* our way to the *feeling* we're after.

My sister is the director of a well-respected career counseling program at a large university. We were talking recently about a career development class she teaches and a unique approach she takes with her students. Adapting something she picked up from author and sociologist Martha Beck, she spends at least a few classes early in the semester on feelings. That's right, feelings. Prefacing the lessons by saying, of course, they'll be digging into resumes and networking and job searches and all the other nuts and bolts of career building. But first, she asserts they dig into feeling. Why? Because in order to make the most authentic and well informed external choices there's a need to tune in internally to what feels good and what feels bad.

If I can't recognize when my mind and body are telling me "no" then I'm likely to just begin a cycle of unhealthy – and unhappy – career and life choices. I'm likely to make choice after choice based on an external sense of "should" rather than a true internal sense of "yes." So, my sister spends time taking her students through exercises to begin to identify what a true yes and a true no feels like for each of them individually; to feel that, not to think about it. The best – and most effective – conversations about practical things like career choices often come from a sense of knowing what something feeling right feels like for you. Having that awareness creates the safe space for the exploration, the trying, and for the wide-open curiosity that leads to the most authentic choices.

I've extrapolated a bit beyond my sister's intentions here to make my point, but like I've talked about elsewhere in these pages, this authenticity of feeling she's helping empower students to dial into and claim has identifiable elements physically, mentally, and emotionally. How am I breathing, sitting, standing, walking, talking etc. when I feel a hard "no" or a passionate "yes"? The more I develop and refine this awareness, the more comfortable and confident I feel in all my choices.

Too often I find we try to start with some pragmatic, well-defined 10-step plan or something. Plans and blueprints are great, but if they are not grounded in a clear sense of what the feeling behind the goal is, then more often than not, in my experience, they are likely not to work. Or if they do work, it's like arriving at a mirage of a finish line and looking around going, "Now what? I'm here but this looks and feels pretty much like where I started." Also, there's a not so subtle value in connecting with the feeling you're after. Doing so allows you to periodically check in with where you are and to use those feelings as a compass. You can use them to check in to see where you are, what's already working and generating that feeling, and what might need to change. You're free, without judgment, to alter the plan as you go because following the plan isn't the key anyway – the feelings are.

So, go ahead and make your lists, build your plans, see it clearly, make it more real and clear in your mind; that can all be super helpful. But then feel it – what's behind it – feel what you imagine it will feel like – how you'll breathe, stand, think, walk and talk during and after. Plans are great, but following a great map to Denver because that's what you *think* you *should* do, and then realizing you really want the *feeling* of being at the beach is not the way to happiness. That's just bad math. Your feelings are your friend and some of your greatest tools. Embrace them. Also, let them change too. I know, I know. Seems contradictory. I'm simply proposing you keep your eye on the prize and that the prize isn't actually the prize itself. What can I tell you? Life is full of poetic paradox.

Certainty is a myth. Start with the feeling, plan from there.

Oprah's On the Phone For You

Not long ago I had the honor of giving a talk at Unity North Atlanta Church, a platform from which many of my teaching/speaking heroes have spoken. The talk was called "Oprah's on the Phone for You." I know, aren't you just dying to know what she has to say? I'll explain.

There's this iconic moment from the Oprah show. It's one moment that, whenever there's some retrospective or tribute to her, always comes up. Do you know the moment? Yep. It's the one when she gives away the cars. I'll refresh your memory. It was on the Oprah Winfrey Show and she was going to be giving away some cars, just a few of them, to just a few members of the audience. And by cars, I mean Pontiacs, little ones. I'm not hating on Pontiacs, I'm just saying these weren't Mercedes-Benz she was giving away.

So, she gives away some cars and tells the audience she's given away the cars she said she would. Then, of course, comes the "but wait there's more" moment as Oprah indicates there's one last car to give away. Then a line of assistants pours into the audience handing out these little paper boxes, like the kind takeout comes in. Oprah says something like, "You've been given a box and if that box has a key in it then you've won the car." By the way, I couldn't love the symbolism more, there's a box and there's a key and it's yours to open. Anyway, she says, "Go!" and everyone starts opening their boxes and, of course, everyone has a car key and Oprah starts blissfully freaking out pointing and jumping and yelling to be heard over the ensuing pandemonium, "You get a car! And you get a car! And you get a car! Everybody gets a car!!!" And the people in the audience are losing their minds too and they're jumping up and down and they're crying and they're hugging perfect strangers and they're screaming "Yes! I won a Pontiac!" And I'm wondering what is happening in that moment? I mean, I get it because I'm at home and I'm jumping up and down clapping and crying and screaming, "Yes! I want a car too!" I'm so excited with them. So, I get it, I get the excitement; but I have to ask, what in the world do they think they just won? It's a little bitty car. It's going to break down in like five years. It's not going to be useful at all anymore. It's just a car. But I know that experience.

I know the desperate experience of feeling like, God, if I could just get that *thing* everything would be fine. I just need that *thing* to shift, to make it alright. As I've said here already, I also know that thing never lasts. That's the heart of the myth we're talking about here. The new job doesn't stay the new job, the relationship doesn't stay the relationship, the money doesn't stay the money. They all change. Which lands us back at what do I think that car is going to mean to me? If I have a new car (job, relationship, money), how could I show up to my life differently? If I have a new car (job, relationship, money), how would I *be* different in my life? Because I think that's what I really mean when I'm looking for that new thing, that new car, that new job, that new relationship. I'm looking for a new experience of my life, which incidentally is happening while I'm looking for a new experience of my life.

And I wonder, if in that moment, without even noticing and because I'm a spiritual being having a human experience, and part of the human experience is goal setting, ambition, and desire, I wonder if, in that moment, without even noticing I am suddenly deferring my happiness to my next goal. Does that make sense? On some fundamental level internally I'm saying, "Ok. I'm just going to struggle here until someone comes along and gives me a paper box with a key in it and then everything will be fine." I think that's missing a huge opportunity. I think if what I'm really after is who I'm going to be when I get it, whatever "it" may be, then perhaps it's time to stop deferring to the law of attraction and start referring to a law of attention. Why? Because what I'm putting my attention on could be the real key to transforming my life.

So, this is what I'm talking about when I talk about turning up my experience of joy and authentic happiness. I want to turn the joy up in my life and I feel like the way I turn up the joy in my life is to turn up my experience of now, and I feel like the way *I get in the way* of my experience of now, is by making "now" more about where I'm going rather than where I am. Does that make sense? Good.

See, Oprah's on the phone for you. Oprah's on the phone for you, and what she wants to say to you is stop coveting her stuff! She wants to say to you, stop thinking it's going to get better if only you have a private jet, if only you have guaranteed income, or a relationship like this, or friends like that! She's saying stop that! Oprah's on the phone and she's saying: You get a life! And you get a life! And you get a life! Everybody gets a life!!! And what are you gonna do with that life?! What are you going to do? Are you going to keep waiting for someone to give you a white box with a key in it to your next car that's going to break down in five years? Or are you going to recognize you are the living white box with a key in it? And that the only shift that really needs to happen for you to start turning up joy in your life now is to start recognizing it's already there. Scripture tells us joy cometh in the morning, it doesn't say it wasn't there at night. That's on us.

And I believe if we're really going to release the myth of certainty and begin to fully attend the "Church of What's Happening Now" (if you will) then we *have to* release this notion that the way I want to feel inside of me in my life is somewhere out there down the road and we *get to* start showing up to it as if it's happening now. And I do mean right now, in this moment.

Now obviously, I've not actually talked with Oprah (yet), but it seems to me so many of the great teachings she's offered and so many of the great teachers she has lifted up, echo this theme of being the change, living your most authentic and fulfilling life and starting that now. I think I'm the one (and perhaps you have too) who let myself slip into believing that, instead, she means someday when all the "stuff" of life is theoretically easier. As far as I know, she's darn sure never said that, and I'll bet if you look at whatever great Teachers' wisdom you look to – regardless of who they are – they are not preaching such an approach that is deeply contingent on your externals being ideal either. That's just not how it's done. Seems more likely it happens the other way around, don't you think?

You get a life. We all want you to shine in this life. We want you to experience magnificence in this life. And we don't want you to wait until you get a new car to start.

Certainty is a myth. Oprah wants you to be happy. Starting now.

They Are All Bridge Jobs

Ok, let's make sure we're on the same page first. What's a bridge job? A bridge job, as I understand it, is a way of framing a job as something bridging a gap between two – perhaps more desirable – jobs. In my experience, the term is often used, well frankly, to make me feel better. As in, "Don't worry, it's just a bridge job." Or, "Why not just get a bridge job in the meantime?" The bottom line is it serves two purposes: first, to kind of say don't sweat it, it's only temporary and, second, to say why not enjoy it, it's only temporary.

The thing is, they are all bridge jobs. No, seriously. Pick your hero. Whomever you choose, they are not doing the same job as they were a decade ago or even five years ago. All careers change. All relationships change. And, again, even mountains change. This is liberating stuff y'all! If you know it's not going to stay the same, isn't that a wonderful permission slip to not get overly caught up in the drama or struggle of it? Also, isn't that a call to be even more present to whatever is happening in the moment since it is, in fact, ephemeral?

This makes me think about improvisational theater (improv). I had the great pleasure several years back of taking improv classes with a wonderful group of people. I highly recommend everyone take improv, by the way. Why? Because the key to improv, as I was taught it, isn't about being funny but rather it's about being present, in the moment, listening and feeding your fellow actors so the story can grow. There are two wonderful lessons I carry from my improv experience: 1) Take life more seriously, and 2) Take life less seriously. The first is about being present and bringing a listening mindfulness to the moment. The second is about being playful and vulnerable and letting the moment pass through you and be gone and then showing up even more openly and boldly to the next. Both are as simple and complicated as they sound. Also, both seem like a couple of really useful life lessons don't you think?

Certainty is a myth. Take life more seriously. Also, take life less seriously. They're all bridge jobs.

Are We There Yet?

At the ever-increasing risk of being redundant, I want to be clear here what I'm talking about. When I refer to everything as being a bridge job and assert there is no certainty and everything is fundamentally ephemeral, I am not proposing an end to commitment and/or loyalty. I am not suggesting we quit jobs on a whim, nor am I suggesting we move into some "free love" version of personal relationships – good lord, dating was hard enough for me! On the contrary, I'm a big fan of commitment and have a fiercely – and occasionally self-destructive – loyal streak in me for sure.

What I am suggesting is that we honor that commitment looks different than we thought it did. What I'm suggesting is that we actually strengthen the depth and value of our commitments by shifting our expectations of them. What I'm suggesting is that we shift to committing to the changing, to the dynamic, and not the static nature of our lives. Not just flippantly saying yeah, yeah, I know it's (insert any "it" you'd like) going to change *some* and I'm cool with that. Instead, I'm suggesting actually – joyfully – committing to the adventure of getting on board with this thing now and actually – joyfully – committing to being psyched about changing and growing with it going forward. Committing to change as the essence of the commitment. Make sense? The dynamic nature of all aspects of life is self-evident, but we've been imposing our own desire for certainty on it. I'm suggesting we might find an expansive deepening in meeting life where and as it is, rather than demanding that it be what it is not.

So then, be where you are. Embrace the moment. Love the journey. Easy, right? No, not so much. So how? Notice there is no certainty. Notice everything changes. Accept that fully and you're halfway there because if there's no certainty then I'm called to embrace where I am, knowing for a fact it's not where I'll be. Simple. Not easy, but simple, right? Let's hit it from another angle, because I think we've already laid the groundwork elsewhere in life for doing this joyfully, even artfully.

Let's talk about one of my favorite things: a road trip. I LOVE going on a good long road trip! I have lost track at this point of the thousands upon thousands of miles I've logged doing so. To my mind, there are few experiences that so naturally exemplify the opportunity to love the journey as a road trip does. Let's lay it out like this. Let's say you decide to take a road trip by car from Crabapple, Georgia (where I am as I type this), to Seattle, Washington. You invite your favorite person along for the ride. It's a nice long diagonal across the country and Google just informed me it'd be 2,625 miles. Excellent. This will take some time, right? Of course. You'd likely lay out some daily goals, some mileage targets. You'd also probably pick some fun destinations you'd like to take in along the way (Graceland anyone?). Sure, sure, you'd do both those things too. Then you'd set out. Sweet!

See this is where road trips get good. You set out with a destination, and usually even a time frame, but then, once you embark, you let it unfold. You don't get mad you're not in Seattle the moment you pull out of your driveway. You don't get mad at Nashville or Denver for not being Seattle. You explore, embrace, and even celebrate who *they* are. You drink in big skies and winding roads. You eat at random greasy spoons *and* the local farmers market with equal pleasure. You pull off when you see some crazy roadside attraction sign like "Giant Superman Statue" (actual thing in Metropolis, Illinois by the way) because you find yourself feeling playful and adventurous. You buy a goofy hat and junk food at the tackiest truck stop you've ever seen. You get sunburned and a flat tire or two and you get frustrated with closed roads only to find the detour takes you through the cutest town you would've blown right past otherwise. You rediscover songs you'd forgotten you love and learn new ones singing the wrong lyrics at the top of your lungs, with the windows down, and one hand out dancing the air. You swap stories, stumble into deep truths, and have an epically ridiculous argument or two. You make up. You get completely punch drunk from the travel and laugh until your sides hurt. Finally, you collapse weary and blissed out at the end of the day. When you awake again, sore and a bit groggy, you're not angry you haven't made it to Seattle. You're looking forward to today's adventure. You know you're getting closer all the time to your destination. And, actually, part of you is kind of wishing the trip could go on just a bit longer.

See, on a road trip, progress is enough. The destination is inevitable. And, most importantly, the dynamic and unpredictable nature of the journey *is* the good news; that *is* where the adventure lives. On a road trip, releasing worry over the destination frees you to be where you are. On a road trip, it is the uncertainty itself that adds to the adventure and helps make every moment delightfully sweet (even the bitter ones) and sharing that adventure with our fellow travelers is the very thing that strengthens and deepens our bond. It is the dynamism and unpredictability of the adventure itself that becomes a story worth telling – and hearing – over and over again.

What I'm saying is embracing uncertainty frees us to embrace the adventure of the road trip we're living. Let your destination be how you want to show up to the world, who you want to show up *as*. And then embark and allow the journey to give you a chance to explore the full spectrum, imagined and unimaginable, of how to show up as You as you go along. Take every detour that speaks to your heart along the way.

Certainty is a myth. Road trips rock. You're right on time.

The Gift of Crappy Gigs

There is a line from a Rudyard Kipling poem I seem to forever be attempting to quote and, more often than not, forgetting how it actually goes. The line is from his poem entitled "If--" and I apologize for so indelicately truncating it here. The line goes like this:

> "...If you can meet triumph and disaster
> And treat those two imposters just the same...
> ...Yours is the Earth and everything that's in it,
> And – which is more – you'll be a Man, my son!"

For me, this sentiment is deeply interwoven into the liberating gift that releasing the myth of certainty has to offer. When I allow myself to embrace the notion that good and bad are labels I'm assigning and, therefore, choices I'm making and choosing to live, I create space for choosing again. I create room to experience life more fully by not deciding what it means categorically.

Speaking of categories. I'm an introvert. Not a classic introvert, obviously, more of what I've heard referenced as a creative introvert. The name doesn't matter. I'm sensitive, deeply empathetic, and sometimes painfully shy, and I need lots of alone time to restore myself. So, of course, I decided a career in the performing arts was the place for me – haha. Here's the great gift I unintentionally began giving myself over twenty years ago: crappy gigs. When you're traveling the country sharing songs and stories and speeches there is a crazy rollercoaster of lonely followed by overwhelming connectedness, followed by lonely, and back again. There is night after night, day after day, of putting your deepest joys, struggles, scars, and dreams out on the table for the whole world to see. There is a dizzying array of rejection and adulation. It's disproportionate, and can be extreme – deifying to crucifying and back again, over and again. It's amazing. It's excruciating. So, wait, how is it a gift? Because either you go insane from listening to and internalizing it all or – more pleasurably – you quickly learn it has very little to do with you. Again, "...if you can meet triumph and disaster – and treat those two imposters just the same..."

The times when I'm able to truly embrace that truth liberate me to show up fully to my craft, to show up fully as me, without needing someone to respond in any particular way. In the end, it's not really about their response, but rather it's about my response to my own inner voice urging me to enter the world in this way. That's the point. Regardless of what your "thing" is.

There's a great line from the iconic Stephen Sondheim musical *Sunday in the Park with George* that goes like this: "Whatever you do / let it come from you / then it will be true / give us more to see." Somewhere over the years of hocking CDs, books, t-shirts and underwear (yes, underwear) from stage after stage, I stopped caring about the stuff as much as I care about the simple and profound gift of the chance to show up fully as me, to swim around in this beautiful moment 'til my fingers get pruney. That's the gift for which I'm so grateful to all the crappy gigs (and the great ones for that matter). That's the gift I offer you. Whether you buy the "record" or not, love it or think it's crap? Well, that's really none of my business. Perhaps, that's the point anyway. Let it go. Show up to your own truth. Give us more to see.

Another quick aside: Perhaps, like many of us, you're not super comfortable embracing that you have something to contribute (I can relate, I'm writing a book at the moment). Maybe it's easier to think whatever you contribute comes from some higher source. Okay. That's fine. Perhaps you are "just" a vessel. But the wine sure doesn't get to the table without a vessel to carry it! That's a pretty critical role in my humble opinion. If it helps, perhaps just try embracing your own vessel-ness a bit more enthusiastically and unapologetically. Give us more to see. And get the wine to the table please, we're thirsty.

I heard this piece on National Public Radio's "My Big Break" series that really struck me. Famed professional rock climber Alex Honnold was talking about the struggle and triumph of being the first person to free climb (without ropes or protection) Yosemite's epic peak Half Dome. I have summited Half Dome – using the trail of course – so maybe that's why the story jumped out at me.

In the story, Alex talks about the intensity of the fear and doubt and focus and flow while working his way to the top of the 2000-foot rock face all alone. He summits and has just had this massive accomplishment. When he gets there, there's the usual array of hikers and tourists who've hiked up the backside of the mountain, a gathering that normally applauds and rushes to congratulate and pose for selfies whenever climbers, wearing the harnesses and safety gear used in traditional climbs, summit. Instead, Alex quietly pulled himself up and arrived at the summit with no such identifying gear on. He emerged triumphant and anonymous, left to revel in his own narrowly eluded disaster and the bliss of what he'd accomplished.

I find this story so powerful and instructive. Rarely is the true nature and gravity of our climb, of our struggles and triumphs, visible. Rarely do our moments of breaking through come with an adoring crowd. But isn't that a gift, or at least an opportunity? To me, it is if I direct my attention away from the desire to say "Hey! What gives?! Don't you get how huge what I just did is? Love me damn it!" To me, the gift is to dig even deeper into the truth that I am called to be my own champion, called to celebrate my own journey, called to share such moments gratefully with my soul and my God. Yes, there may be a close few who will really "get" what you've come through and that sense of being seen is huge, but the real gold is found in *me* getting it, in *me* seeing me. That's where I become triumphant.

My point is be your own witness, be your own champion. As a life coach and, really, even in my normal interactions with friends and/or strangers, I find often times we just hunger for a witness. Sometimes we're looking for a witness to see us as we see ourselves, our best selves. Sometimes we're hungry for a witness to affirm and celebrate our accomplishments or mourn with us in our losses. I get that. I feel that too. The thing is, some – if not many – of the hardest things you and I have been through, I mean the moments you thought might really do you in, I'm willing to bet you went through alone. These are moments no one will ever truly understand. But why in the world should that diminish their value? The more I show up fully to now, to the moments of my life, the more I feel called to be my own witness. I feel called to release the need for a crowd of tourists that applauds, rushes to congratulate me and asks to pose for selfies. I feel called to be my own champion, to stand arms wide and declare my summit with my own barbaric yawp! That is enough.

Certainty is a myth. You rock, but you knew that already.

Beauty Everywhere

This is another habit I've gotten into since I've returned to retail. As I alluded to earlier, I make it a point to notice something in the parking lot every day I find to be beautiful. Often times I'll post a picture to my social media feeds. It could be a tree, clouds, sunrise, or maybe a shadow. The thing doesn't matter. Noticing it does. You've probably noticed so much of what we've explored so far comes back to perspective or rather to the law of attention I mentioned earlier. This gets back to a very basic and powerful axiom: feed what you want to grow. I find this to be so very true, both literally and figuratively, and easily one of the most powerful gifts of my daily practice.

There *is* beauty everywhere if I'm looking for it. There is also ugly if I'm looking for that. Which do I want to see? Which one serves me in how I want to show up in the world, in being whom I want to show up in the world as? Does it serve me more to see beauty in the places and in the people I encounter in my life? Or is my life made more rich and full focusing on the ugly side of things? Everything and everyone, in my experience has both in them. Remember the color exercise earlier? That's what I'm talking about again here, choosing and then feeding what you want to see, what you want to grow.

How does releasing the myth of certainty fit in here? Well, again, the more I release my attachment to outcome and the more in the moment I am, the more beauty I see and the more gratitude I feel. Gratitude. There's something I haven't dwelled on much specifically which is a shame, and needs rectifying. Actually, I don't need to go on about this too much. It's simple, really. If there's only one tool you start using after reading this, one tool that will absolutely transform your life as soon as you start using it regularly, begin practicing gratitude. Offer gratitude in your mind, heart, and – better – out loud, for everything as your attention falls on it. Gratitude for the breeze, for your partner, for a green light, for a red light, for the sun, the clouds, the rain, for waking up this morning. I cannot overstate the impact and lift brought by the simple act of giving thanks. Gratitude is the fertilizer in the "feed what you want to grow" soil. Practice gratitude. Enough said.

Practically speaking, another great way of beginning to feed what you want to grow can begin at the end of the day today. Sometimes I look back over my day and lament all I didn't get done or the things I wish I hadn't done. And by sometimes, I mean, until recently, every day. Well, that's not helpful. It's particularly not helpful when I'm conscious of what I'm, therefore, feeding. So, something that's working for me is directing my attention to what I *did* do that day, what I *am* proud of. I've actually begun practicing this throughout the day and, most importantly, when I'm talking about my day with loved ones or even strangers. When I'm characterizing my day to someone else, I get to choose what to share, right? Well, what possible value – in terms of what I want to grow – is there to be found in lamenting, complaining and highlighting what I'm not pleased with? I think when I focus on and share what's working, what I'm grateful for, what I'm proud of, I'm essentially building myself up and sending a message clearly and loudly to the Universe: "More like that please!"

Incidentally, that last phrase "More like that please!" is also a very consistent and empowering part of my gratitude and faith practice. I like to think God wants for me what I want for me. Actually, I like to think God is kind of like my personal chef. Any personal chef worth their salt wants you to love what they make for you, right? Also, no personal chef worth their salt is going to ask you how to make it for you, right? So, relieved of the job of figuring out how to make it happen, I like to make sure to call out the "ingredients" I'm learning I love as I go with a hearty, "More like that please!" Then comes the *Where's Waldo?* fun part of just keeping my eyes open to notice how that ingredient is showing up more and more in the bounty before me. And to then offer gratitude, of course.

This practice is just like the color exercise from earlier but with the added potency of intention and gratitude. See and feel something you want more of in your world? Claim it as such. Call it out. More like that please! Then actively look for and notice how it starts showing up in your life and/or how it was there already. Repeat often.

Certainty is a myth. Feed what you want to grow.

Truth or Consequences

aka Why Bother?

At this point, this all may seem a bit cerebral and you may have some good ole "yeah buts" popping up. You may even be asking why bother? Well, like I said earlier I think my tendency to "yeah but" can be self-defeating, but also can be a powerful tool directing my attention to deeply held beliefs and subtle internal currents. So, let's give this question of "Why bother?" some ink.

I think, in general and certainly when it comes to the myth of certainty, our problem is with the invisible. Mental and emotional discomfort - regardless of the degree - are invisible. Therefore, we seem to believe they shouldn't be something that is deserving of time and attention. However, a flat tire? Runny nose? Cut? Even soreness after a long day at work? These things are all visible, and we don't blink at them being addressed appropriately. How much more exponential would our growth be in terms of confidence, self-esteem, and competence if we listened to those inner voices and addressed our emotional and mental needs with the same level of compassion, understanding, and intention? What if we somehow made the invisible visible? Would that empower us to address them differently?

What does that have to do with uncertainty? We've made uncertainty our enemy because it's uncomfortable and because it's uncomfortable in a way we can't see or address immediately in the physical. As I write this, the United Kingdom is sorting through the fallout over the so-called "Brexit" vote to leave the European Union. I know this is a very specific and seemingly random example, but bear with me. I was watching the news the other night and they were interviewing a global financial markets expert who was expressing her dismay over the state of things. Her principle point – true story – was that there's a great deal of uncertainty and the markets don't like uncertainty. This is my point also.

We have made certainty (which everything in our actual experience of life tells us is simply not an attainable goal) the enemy of uncertainty (which everything in our actual experience of life tells us is simply the natural state of the world). So, we've made the one thing we know is going to be consistently true and active in our lives the constant the enemy of everything we claim we want. Read those two sentences again. No, seriously, please read them again. Do you see a paradigm problem? I feel like we need a new approach.

I like to play blackjack. I'm not saying I'm great at it, I'm just saying I like to play it. Any amateur or pro gambler will tell you the same thing: the house always wins. It's just math. You can change the way you play, the way you bet and such, to make it more likely you'll leave the table with as much or maybe more than you sat down with, but sooner or later the stats will catch up with you and the house will win. The myth of certainty is like that, and we keep placing the wrong bet. We know for sure uncertainty runs this house, but we sit down time and again, go all in, the house wins and we get up broke, crushed, disillusioned and yet mystifyingly chomping at the bit to get back in the game and confident we can win the next time. Stop that! It's a bad bet!

So, why bother? Why bother trying to embrace uncertainty instead? Because we've been asking the wrong question.

We've been asking time and again how to outsmart the house. We've been trying time and again to outsmart uncertainty in our relationships, jobs, health, and on and on. We've been under the impression we're engaged in some epic rivalry while uncertainty sits confidently, unaware we're even rivals. Certainty *is* a myth. Embracing that reality liberates us from continuing to force certainty onto an inherently uncertain universe. This liberation is not a defeat. As I've been endeavoring to illustrate, liberation from the myth of certainty frees us to show up to and embrace more fully what is. Actually, in many ways it allows us to more fully live the hope and trust – the faith, if you will – that has caused us to sit at the table and place our losing bets. The faith that it will all work out. The faith it is already working out. We show up and we trust.

Certainty is a myth. Bet on it.

Doubt

Okay, what about doubt? Knowing something is going to be uncomfortable and embracing it are different things. Feelings are tricky, though, as I've said, very useful. I'm all for feeling all the feels. I'm of the belief my emotions, my feelings, tell me where I am not who I am. All too often I get caught up in those transitory emotions as if they are somehow who I am. Remember, part of the good news in embracing uncertainty is you're no longer prisoner of the illusion that discomfort is here to stay. Knowing that is the key.

So, I think there are a couple of things worth digging into and remembering here. First, the seasons. I often comment, usually during the winter months, regardless of how insulated and comfortable – relatively speaking –most of us in technologically advanced nations find ourselves, we are still subject to the seasons. Here's a post from my Facebook feed back in January,

> "Gently remember, the seasons are within you as well as around you. Allow that. Burrow in. Be loving and gentle with yourself.
>
> As I write this, I'm listening to a peaceful piano playlist on Spotify, a space heater is warming my room to a cozy embrace, a candle, with the visage of the Buddha that I find so soothing, flickers softly on my desk. I'm looking out the window through

> sleet and barren trees at a grey January sky. Why in the world – regardless of the abundance of my indoor perch – why in the world should I expect my head and heart to not feel some of that same barren and damp cold?
>
> I get heavy, quiet, and introspective this time of year. So, does all of life it seems. Perhaps that's a clue I'm not broken or off track in my quiet malaise. Perhaps it's a call to recess, to retreat. I've always loved recess and retreats. Why not embrace the opportunity winter calls me to?"

The reason I felt that was worth sharing here is that it's okay, and right on time, to feel whatever you're feeling, whenever you feel it. It's a natural part of the flow of life. We're the ones who have pitted ourselves against it. Part of the gift of embracing the fluidity and uncertainty of life is allowing ourselves to experience, and move through, seasons of doubt, joy, hope, etc. knowing we're exactly who and where we're supposed to be and the seasons within will change soon enough. Inevitably. Seems to work for the trees.

The second point I want to offer in dealing with discomfort and doubt – and joy for that matter – drills down a bit further on this notion that feelings tell us where we are not who we are. Like I said, I'm all about feeling all the feelings. It's not about denying what you're feeling, it's about choosing what you're feeding.

I was remembering recently the experience of Easter morning. I grew up Catholic, so Easter was a big deal, but I'm actually not talking about that side of Easter here. I'm talking about the Easter Bunny end of things. Evidently, the Easter Bunny provided my parents with a map of where he'd hidden everything because they always knew. My brother, sister and I would dash around the house trying to find what the mischievous oversized rabbit had left behind. I remember my folks either sitting on the couch, or coming to find each of us in some far off closet we had wandered off to searching diligently. They'd start giving us hints saying, "You're warm, warmer. Nope now you're cold, colder, icy, you're Antarctica." Things like that. Did this happen in your house? Anyway, the gold of course was, "You're getting warm, warmer, hot, burning up, how are you not on fire?!" Tada! I found it!

Feelings are like this when I embrace them. Regardless of what area of my life I'm in while working through something, if I can be brave enough to embrace the feelings that arise, they are very often showing me where to go. Icy? Turn back. Warmer? Go forward. Icy, but in a good way? Listen closer, perhaps there's some important discomfort to go through. Make sense? And, not for nothing, sometimes the most uncomfortable feelings are there, like the most bitter taste you can imagine, to make it clear to us what we do and do not want by providing a stark and extreme contrast. Contrast is cool like that.

So go ahead and doubt. Go ahead and believe with irrational fervor. Go ahead and feel all the feelings. Be gentle and compassionate with yourself. Feelings are not always easy, but they are never a sign you are broken. They are a reminder you are part of the flow, and they are your guides showing you to the next "right" turn on your journey.

Certainty is a myth. Feelings are a gift. All of them.

But the Trees Are So Beguiling

It's perhaps the most cliché of clichés. Used in a myriad of contexts it is simply "she/he can't see the forest for the trees." The notion, I suppose, is the individual trees themselves so captivate one's attention that one loses sight of the bigger picture, the broader context. In this case, that the tree is only a small part of a presumably vast forest. I get this. I have a deep love for trees – metaphorical and otherwise. As I type this, I'm perched (intentionally) in a chair by a window overlooking a beautiful and majestic old oak tree. Interestingly, I just now noticed there are a number of other trees I've been ignoring between here and the stately old one I've been admiring in the hours and days I've written here. Ha! I guess that proves the point quite literally.

Also interesting to me is the definition of the word beguiling. I'm a big fan (or nerd) of looking up words I have any question about – thank god for apps! Anyway, for kicks I looked up beguiling when I decided to use it in the title of this section. Lo and behold, the definition includes most of the sort of romantic and enchanting connotations I had intended, but it also has denotations of trickery, cheating and/or deceiving. Nice. That works too. Let's dig in.

I'll own this. I can't see the forest for the trees. When meeting someone new, the myth of certainty paradigm we've been talking about plays out like this:

"Hey, I want to introduce you to Brian.

Hey Brian. Nice to meet you. What do you do?

I *am* a ___________..."

It's this "I am-ness" I/we are so hung up on that gets me into trouble. When I "I am" myself and attach myself to some external job or status, I am tying myself to one tree and ignoring the forest. Put another way, I am self-identifying with something I know – because I'm starting to embrace the gifts of uncertainty – will absolutely change. On some fundamental level doesn't that mean that I'm defining myself by something unreal and, therefore, untrue? Bear with me. This is more than semantics.

The trees *are* beguiling and we should honor and celebrate that. Enjoying the ports and positions, relationships and revolutions along the journey is a huge part of the learning and the reason for embarking. My point isn't to skip that. Let me come at this from a different angle. The quarterback for the NFL team the Carolina Panthers, Cam Newton, had this tradition of giving the football to a young fan after a touchdown. There was this moment during the 2015 season that was caught on camera of him leaping up into the stands to give a ball to a little girl, decked out in Carolina gear, who seemed to be at the game with her family. I watched this video over and over again. This little girl's reaction to the moment just left me speechless. When I shared the link with my partner she gave me the words immediately. She smiled and laughed and said something like, "That's amazing! The look on her face is like she's thinking 'I've peaked!'" That is absolutely the look! Of course, it's safe to assume she hasn't, in fact, peaked. And that's the point.

Sometimes when I "I am" myself, I'm attaching to something as if I'm saying that I've peaked, or bottomed out. You haven't. If you're alive, you haven't peaked, and you're not broken. You're in it now, getting to show up anew right now. It's great to celebrate moments that feel good and to mourn in moments that are full of anguish. The key is not to move into or set up shop in either of them. Feel them. Be with them. Honor them. Then pull back the lens you're looking through and remember it's a tree, not the whole forest. You are both. Both/and moments are complex, sure, but also healing. There is more to see. There is more to be.

Certainty is a myth. You are the forest and the tree.

Answer the Call

So what then? If I start embracing uncertainty, what does my "I am-ness" look like?

Earlier, we talked a bit about faith and I asserted that we're all exercising some degree of faith by virtue of where we direct our attention and in what truths we ground our beliefs. Part of the appeal of many, if not most, organized religions is not just that they provide a blueprint for behaving in this life, but also that they offer the promise of a utopian afterlife or the threat of a nightmarish hell. I don't know about an afterlife, maybe there is one and maybe there isn't. I do know there's this whole amazing place to be in right now. I do know about this life and I do know the feeling of the experience of what I'd call heaven and of what I'd call hell.

Very briefly, let's look at heaven and hell as we live them in this life. Have you ever gone through a very difficult and painful experience during which you said something to the extent of, "I'm going through a special kind of hell"? Yeah, me too. Have you ever had wonderful experience, a magnificent experience even, during which you found yourself going (in a sing-song-y voice), "Oh…I'm in heaven!" Yeah, me too. So we know when we're talking about the experience of heaven and hell we're, once again, talking about a set of feelings. We know what it feels like. Let's drill down on that. What does it feel like when I'm going through hell? When I'm going through hell I feel disconnected. I feel isolated. I feel disconnected from a sense of hope, from a sense of purpose. I feel lost and lonely. I feel so many things that, when I look at them, boil down to feeling disconnected. When I'm feeling like I'm in heaven, I feel connected. I might feel connected to a sunset. I might feel connected to a song. I might feel connected to another person. I might feel connected to a sense of purpose or in the flow, but it's a sense of connection that is the hallmark of my experience of heaven. You could say it's a sense of feeling myself as both the tree and the forest from earlier. It's this connection, this sense of relatedness that feels like heaven.

My friend Reverend Richard from early in these pages said something that has stuck with me. He said joy is relational. Hmmm. I get that. Joy *is* relational. It is about the relationship I choose to take with the experiences of my life. About stepping into claiming that relationship, being intentional about it. Once again, like when I encounter people sharing the same external experiences, e.g. wealth or poverty, single or married, but showing up to those experiences profoundly different. It's clear to me, there is a choice being made, a call being answered.

What's the call? The call is to choose to show up *as* you, to show up in the world and to the minutia of your life as the highest version of who *you* want to be. The call is to *be* your heaven now. The call is to stop measuring yourself and your life experiences solely by some worldly yardstick mired in an illusion of certainty. The goal is to measure yourself by something more akin to a godly yardstick, an internal sense of your own authenticity, your own truest and most loving path. Show up to your life like that.

By the way, one empowering element of that "godly yardstick" is my/your ability to bring a greater consciousness, a deeper awareness, to the thoughts rattling around my head and to the words coming out of my mouth. What version of me am I feeding energy and power to? What elements of me am I emphasizing and, therefore, growing? At the joyful risk of oversimplifying this, if I want to grow a rose garden but instead I am continually planting, fertilizing and watering marigolds what's going to grow? Exactly. I've said it before and I'll say it many, many times in the future. You are mighty. Repeatedly emphasizing and sharing the parts of you that you want to grow and prosper in your life – and thereby feeding and watering them – is just one aspect of the mightiness of you waiting for you on the other side of you answering the call.

So how do you answer the question, "Nice to meet you! What do you do?" Well, go ahead and tell them what you do. Just don't forget to include what you *really* do, what you want to feed, who you *really* Be. Go ahead and name your profession if you'd like, but then add something like, "That's what they call what I do but what I really love about what I do is how it feels to _______, or getting to _______, or the satisfaction of ________, or it allows me to spend more time ________." Why not own what you really get out of the settings you choose to call home in this life? Or pivot entirely and don't talk about work at all and instead share something cherished that you're growing. Perhaps talk about how passionate you are about bringing/being more _______ in the world. Your answer. Your call. (And vice versa.) By the way, a person who answered along those lines is someone I'd want to meet, wouldn't you?

Certainty is a myth. Go to heaven.

Simple Not Easy

A few months ago, driving home from work I passed a small church with one of those marquis with the pop-in letters. It was after dark and I was on the phone with my best friend. The sign, bright against the night, was announcing an upcoming funeral. It read: "CELEBRATING THE LIFE OF BRIAN PERRY." I nearly drove off the road and I certainly cursed – profusely – into the phone. That rattled me good. But it also got me thinking, am I? Am I celebrating the life of Brian Perry or am I struggling through it? Am I suffering through the life of Brian Perry? The urgent desire to celebrate more and suffer less is, I think, ultimately what got me out of my own way long enough to share these thoughts at all.

Certainty is a myth and that *is* great news. It is news that can liberate me from the incessant need to be striving for the next goal, investing my sense of worth exclusively in my next accomplishment. Poetically, doing so also frees me to be more present to and get more joy out of the experience of striving as well.

So, will these changes happen overnight? I mean, what's next? Well, lots of practice but not the kind of practice that happens behind closed doors. More like becoming a better swimmer by splashing around in the pool as your strokes form and gradually improve. But you get to swim the whole time! Yay! So, you begin by beginning. You do by doing. Simple not easy.

A couple of final thoughts. Derek Sivers, founder of CDBaby.com (and now to be found at sivers.org), is a bit of a business guru in my world. He talks in multiple articles about the importance of version 0.1, lamenting that far too many amazing and beautiful ideas are lost on their way to a grand unveiling of Version 1.0 – tada! He argues the trick is to share version 0.0 then 0.1 then 0.2 and so on. Along the way to version 1.0, not only are you likely to receive invaluable feedback that allows you to make, hone, and craft increasingly better versions of whatever you're creating, but also by the time you're ready to unveil Version 1.0 you'll have a community of believers and advocates already in your corner.

This, by the way, I find is one of the great perks of pursuing songwriting. The way you succeed as a songwriter is by writing great songs. The way you write great songs is by writing songs. The goal of succeeding is to be able to write songs all the time. The way you succeed is by writing songs as often as possible. I believe that's what's known as a win-win. Embracing uncertainty and turning the joy up, the experience of now up, in your life is like that too. You do it by doing it.

I have a friend who was recently talking about a career goal involving speaking/podcasts/radio show type of thing. I asked her,

"Clearly there must be people who are making a career out of this and loving it?"

"Yeah, but they've been doing it like 20 years."

"Right. But doesn't that mean that 20 years ago they started?"

This holds true for personal aspirations as well. Let's take relationships. Let's say you're looking for someone with whom to share your life. Let's say you're fantasizing about long walks, movies, dinners at groovy restaurants, travel, breakfast in bed, etc. Aren't those things you can be doing now? I mean it. All of them are, aren't they? And who's more attractive to you?

A) Someone who's waiting for someone to come along and "complete" them.

B) Someone who's confidently, joyfully living a life as a complete person who they'd love to share with someone else.

I've got to go with B every time. And what do you have to lose? Worst-case scenario, you do things you love doing and occasionally feel a yearning or loneliness even while doing them. I'm not making light of that. I've lived that and, in my experience, it can be excruciating. You know what's worse? The loneliness without any of the joy and adventure. The waiting for someone's arrival without working on embracing and celebrating my *own* arrival.

Also, my experience of how Life/the Universe/God works is that when I do what I can with what I have from where I am, the Universe responds exponentially. What I focus on grows and, out of that focus and growth, more opportunities to do/be things I love arise.

The basic question is whether I'm deferring my experience and expression of my ideal self until such time as I find myself in the ideal circumstances I imagine? If so, and knowing uncertainty will always prevail and circumstances will always change, wouldn't it be more fun to start thinking, talking, behaving, and feeling the experience and expression of my ideal self now? Simple not easy.

Perspective. Use it to your advantage.

A friend asked me, "So you're basically talking about brainwashing yourself?"

Well. Yes. But, again, we do that anyway in choosing our perspective – our beliefs – about life. I'm suggesting if you're going to be brainwashed why not do it yourself and wash away the parts that aren't serving you? Isn't that sort of the overall goal of washing anyway? Think of it as a twist on the ever popular social media phenomenon "Throwback Thursday," if you want. Instead of dredging up something old to revisit you throwback something that you no longer wish to carry, that no longer serves you.

Start by starting. Begin by beginning. Can you spare five minutes a day? A week? To do something that turns you on and brings you joy? Sure you can. You have a timer in your pocket right now. It's on your phone. Set it and go. Stop when it goes off. I mean it, stop. Try that for a while and direct your attention to what changes. Again, arguably the most impactful thing I've ever done requires five minutes a week and a $5 paint pen.

The paradigm shift I am calling myself to here, the shift I have done my best to articulate within these pages, is a fundamental shift in the ways I/we measure the experiences of life. In light of the knowledge of the mythical nature of certainty; in beginning to accept the futility of striving for such certainty, the measure of an experience cannot be simply the illusory achievements and destinations along the way. The measure of the experience of my life must begin to find its way instead to an emphasis on how I show up to my life – how I think, speak, and behave – passing through the smallest and greatest so-called watershed moments of my life. How much love and joy, kindness and compassion, openness and gratitude am I *being* in those moments? In an unavoidably uncertain world, that's the true measure of the experience.

Simple isn't necessarily small. That's what I'm learning. Simple isn't easy either. Simple is, however, the answer. And it just takes practice. Everything you've ever gotten great at and loved doing took practice. Some practice sessions were more fun than others, sure, but at its core, the practice was joyful. The practice we're speaking of here is with your life, with how you show up in the world. Practicing – consciously, intentionally – who you are in the world.

My goal in these pages was not to give you the impression that doing any or all of the things herein will make it all *feel* better. Rather, my hope is to relieve you of the notion that your feelings are your enemy. To give you tools to remember that you can show up now as who you've been dreaming of being someday. With practice. If any of the thoughts/tools here resonate with you, my guess is you'll remember to use them sometimes and forget them totally and completely at other times. That is to say, that's my guess if you're anything like me.

Simple not easy. Remind yourself of this as you practice. Say it out loud. This work we're engaged in, this paradigm shift we've embarked upon is simple. Simple but not easy. We are – all of us – making this up as we go. That is how it is done and how it has always been done.

Taking a break in the moments before writing these last lines, I headed over to my Facebook feed. There was a post from one of my favorite souls, Elizabeth Gilbert, discussing a major shift in the certainty of her world. In describing it she wrote these words, "I trust that you understand that this is a story that I am living – not a story I am telling."

This is, as Miss Gilbert said so poetically, a story that I am living – not a story I am telling. These musings are the truths I feel at this moment in time. This is what's working for me. I hope, future Brian or dear Reader, should these words find you, that they will lift you into more of you. You are a gift beyond measure. Shine.

Certainty is a myth. Begin.

Epilogue

Hell In a Hand Basket? Not If You Can Help It.

This book is very centered on personal change. That may come off as a bit tone-deaf at the moment. As I write this, there's the perception in the public at large that we live in an increasingly violent and uncertain world. There's a palpable sense of fear and a desperate hunger for answers. I think that's a function of both actual events and the immediacy of access, and inherent biases, of information through social media and the 24-hour news cycle. In other words, while certainly disturbing and unacceptable things have happened, our experience of the fear and uncertainty is intensified by our current approach to disseminating and receiving information. Nevertheless, I felt like it was important to add a passage here to speak to the experience of wanting the world at large to change.

This book *is* very centered on personal change. There's a reason for that. The reason is that I am passionate about changing the world for the better. It's personal.

It's true, at least in the circles I'm in, that of late, there's been an increasing sense of frustration, anxiety, fear, sadness, division, justified outrage, despair and really just this pervasive sense of helplessness to change things. I want to honor that and to share what's working for me as I've been actively seeking to disavow myself of the notion that I am, in fact, helpless.

I want to start in a place that may annoy you a bit, but was a huge ah-ha for me as I caught myself bemoaning the state of *the* world, looking out at *the* world and how it seems to be devolving and so deeply troubled. I thought, well, hold up. *The* world is also *my* world. I'm also in and of that world, and in some really meaningful ways, that is me. I'm part of the world. This is me I'm talking about as I'm bemoaning the state of it. And in these times it can be very easy – and very human – for me to want change to happen now, to want a switch to flip and things to change overnight. But you and I both know that's not how sweeping change happens. Sweeping change doesn't happen all at once. More importantly, sweeping cultural change doesn't happen to us. It happens through us.

That brought me back to one of the truths the great teachers have all taught in their own ways for centuries, which was so succinctly expressed in a quote often attributed to Mahatma Gandhi, "You must be the change you wish to see in the world." I think, however, this seemingly global instruction is also very local and specific. I think if I want to see change in *the* world, then I have to be the change in *my* world. I think if I want to see more love, more kindness, more compassion, more nonviolence, more civility, more joy in the world, then I need to be those things in my world. I need to show up to work with more love, to traffic with more kindness, to the grocery store with more compassion, to my family with more civility, to my relationship with more joy, and on and on and on. It can't just be about throwing up competing facts on social media and trying to forcefully change people's minds.

It is about living my life differently. It's about bringing the values I want to see in the world to the world through me. It's about doing the thing that's simple but not easy. Change doesn't happen to us, it happens through us. And I think the call for us, in these challenging times, is to show up to that, to show up *as* that. To step up to that. To answer the call. To be the change we wish to see in the world.

The great news – as we explored in these pages – is, as you do this thing that's simple but not easy, you get to begin experiencing it in the goings-on in your own life. You're living it after all. So you get to begin experiencing it in *your* world. Until eventually the culture catches up with us.

So, feel the feelings. Keep practicing. Be compassionate and good to you. This is what change looks like. Let me say that again. This *is* what change looks like and that is the gift inside the wrapping of the certainty of uncertainty. Just keep showing up as more and more of you and you are doing it. It is happening. This is what change looks like. All is well.

Certainty is a myth. Be the change you wish to see in *your* world.

References

Notes to help you find your way to some of the inspiring folks I referenced in this book. Each is referenced below by chapter. If you have any further questions, please reach out through yesbrianperry.com.

Dear Reader,

- "It's a bit like you've lost something..." Quote is from the introduction to *The Art of Happiness* which is written by His Holiness The Dalai Lama and Howard C. Cutler, M.D..

Intro

- *The Newsroom* is a television series created by Aaron Sorkin that ran for three wonderful seasons on HBO. The quote I used is from Season 1, Episode 4 that is called "I'll Try to Fix You."

We're All Making This Up

- "Do not be too timid or squeamish..." is attributed to Ralph Waldo Emerson and is evidently from his journal entry dated November 11, 1842.
- This chapter includes my recollection of the experience of hearing the Dalai Lama speak at Emory University in

Atlanta, Georgia, on October 19, 2010. More information regarding His Holiness can be found at dalailama.com.

- "If we listened to our intellect..." Quote from Ray Bradbury is, frankly, attributed to many different originating sources. The one I've used is from an October 1990 interview distributed by the *New York Times News Service.*
- "Fall on your face..." – Quote is from singer/songwriter Gina Forsyth. More information about Gina can be found at ginaforsyth.com.
- "I did not come here to suffer." – Elizabeth Gilbert is the author of numerous books including *Big Magic* and *Eat, Pray, Love.* Incidentally, *Big Magic* is part of what compelled me to take a leap and write this book in the first place. I reference her more than once in these pages. Her website is elizabethgilbert.com.

Turn the Other Cheek
aka Change the Frequency

- Rev. Richard Burdick who is referenced here as well as later in the book is the Spiritual Leader of Unity North Atlanta Church. Information can be found at unitynorth.org.
- "People are disturbed not by things..." Quote is from the *Enchiridion* by Greek Stoic philosopher Epictetus.

Yeah, But

- "Argue for your limitations..." – Quote is from *Illusions: The Adventures of a Reluctant Messiah* (1977) by Richard Bach. His website is richardbach.com.

A Word About a Word

- This chapter includes my recollection of the experience of hearing Marianne Williamson speak on October 17, 2009 at Unity North Atlanta Church in Marietta, Georgia. Marianne Williamson is the author of many books including *A Return to Love* and her website is marianne.com.

Owning Your Power

- "I woke up like this." Is from Beyoncé's song ****Flawless*. It probably doesn't need to be added here in the references but, you know, it's Beyoncé so respect.

Do Anything

- "When you don't know what you want…" Quote is from author and teacher Mike Dooley. More information about his work can be found at TUT.com. Oh, and be sure to sign up for his daily "Notes from the Universe" email. I know I know but trust me you'll be happy to receive *these* emails.

Oprah's On the Phone For You

- The car giveaway I recount happened during the September 13, 2004 episode of *The Orpah Winfrey Show*. Her website is Oprah.com.

The Gift of Crappy Gigs

- "…If you can meet triumph and disaster..." – Quote is from Rudyard Kipling's poem entitled *If--*.
- "Whatever you do/let it come from you…" – Quote is from Stephen Sondheim's musical *Sunday in the Park with George*.

- The story I used regarding Alex Honnold's Half Dome ascent is from the January 3, 2016 edition of National Public Radio's series *My Big Break* and can be found on npr.org. For more information on Alex Honnold, visit alexhonnold.com.

Simple Not Easy

- As I mentioned within the text, more information and insight from Derek Sivers can be found at sivers.org.

Epilogue:
Hell In a Hand Basket? Not If You Can Help It.

- "You must be the change..." So, this one threw me a bit. Evidently, there's some disagreement over who originally said this iconic quote and whether Mahatma Gandhi ever said it all. In the absence of what I found to be a credible consensus and given my use of it here was to represent a commonly taught philosophy, I chose to present it here as often attributed to Mahatma Gandhi.